PRAISE FOR *USING CREA*
AND DATA IN MARKETI...

Logic and magic seem like they belong to separate worlds. But it is their unique combination that creates massive impact. Tom Ollerton understands this and goes on to explain it in an integrated fashion – with evidence, with facts, with stories, with anecdotes. This book informs, inspires and, importantly, makes you think. Many authors attempt to solve the problem. Very few try to provoke better solutions. If you want the latter, you are reading the right book.

Aparna Sundaresh, Global Chief Marketing Officer, De'Longhi Group

Using Creativity with Data is a sharp, timely exploration of how marketers can turn data from a blunt instrument into a creative superpower. It reflects what I believe in: marketing that's culturally curious, emotionally resonant and insight-led. This book is for anyone who wants to build brands with purpose, precision, and imagination

Arjoon Bose, Global Chief Marketing & Digital Officer, Bel

As Gen AI boosts efficiency, marketers who fail to harness data for creative insights and inspiration will be left behind. Tom Ollerton draws on real-world examples from seasoned leaders to demonstrate how data can fuel, not stifle, impactful work. Essential reading for those aiming to drive business growth through the blending of data and creativity

Lisa Delaney, Regional Head of Marketing and Lifestyle – Europe, Cathay Pacific

Tom's lived this tension first-hand, and it shows. This is an inspiring, practical read for anyone trying to unlock creativity at scale. Use data to be relevant to more people, not visible to fewer – and let empathy, not just efficiency, guide your marketing. It's a book that earns your attention.

Jerry Daykin, Head of International Media, Restaurant Brands International

Like a renaissance polymath, Tom Ollerton beautifully orchestrates how art and science must coexist to drive the best pieces of innovation. Only by being genuinely curious and having your audiences as a starting point, that can new assertive possibilities be presented. Leveraging the right data combined with human-centric strategies is the only path to produce a masterpiece.

Michelle Urdiales, CMO Latin America, Maersk

In a world overwhelmed by data and performance metrics, creativity is under attack. Through case studies and interviews with brands and leading industry voices this book deftly navigates and acknowledges the real challenge: how to control, understand and humanise your data to unleash creativity – not constrain it – putting marketing firmly back in the driver's seat.

Adam Boita, CMO, Ecologi

Tom Ollerton's Creative Marketing in a Data Driven Age is the antidote to the endless 'data is king' decks we've all endured. It's a confident, no-nonsense playbook that proves data alone isn't enough - creative interpretation is the real unlock that makes campaigns catch fire. Bold, practical and ahead of the curve, he challenges tired marketing orthodoxy and delivers actionable inspiration by the bucketload.

Scott Somerville, Director of External Affairs, E.On

As marketers we often feel that data dictates our creative campaigns rather than enhances it. But how do you turn this on its head? *Using Creativity and Data in Marketing* will be the reset button you've been looking for. The book offers invaluable insights into how data can inspire and enhance creative ideas, rather than limit them. From better understanding your target customer, writing better briefs, building effective teams, and measuring success meaningfully, the book is packed with real-world examples and contributions from industry leaders. Unlock the full potential of data-driven creativity that helps you to create stand-out campaigns that you, and your boss, were looking for!

Jasper Martens, Chief Marketing Officer, PensionBee

Using Creativity and Data in Marketing

Unlocking creative value
with insight and imagination

Tom Ollerton

KoganPage

First published in Great Britain in 2025 by Kogan Page Limited

Kogan Page
Kogan Page Ltd, 2nd Floor, 45 Gee Street, London EC1V 3RS, United Kingdom
Kogan Page Inc, 8 W 38th Street, Suite 902, New York, NY 10018, USA
www.koganpage.com

EU Representative (GPSR)
Authorised Rep Compliance Ltd, Ground Floor, 71 Baggot Street Lower, Dublin D02 P593, Ireland
www.arccompliance.com

Kogan Page books are printed on paper from sustainable forests.

The right of the authors to be identified as the author of this work has been asserted by him in accordance with the Copyright, Designs and Patents Act 1988.

ISBNs
Hardback   978 1 3986 1927 2
Paperback   978 1 3986 1925 8
Ebook   978 1 3986 1926 5

British Library Cataloguing-in-Publication Data
A CIP record for this book is available from the British Library.

Library of Congress Cataloging-in-Publication Data
2025940650

Typeset by Integra Software Services, Pondicherry
Print production managed by Jellyfish
Printed and bound by CPI Group (UK) Ltd, Croydon, CR0 4YY

To Fanni and Lola,
the two people who couldn't care less about marketing
and two people I couldn't care about more

CONTENTS

ABOUT THE AUTHOR

Tom Ollerton is the Founder of Automated Creative, the only strategically led dynamic ad platform that inspires clients' future creative.

Since 2018, Automated Creative has made and optimized ad creatives using live data and insight globally for brands like Bose, MARS, McDonald's, Mastercard, AMEX, Amazon, Bausch + Lomb, Brown-Forman, Suntory Global Spirits, Crocs, Formula 1, Lipton, Diageo, Miele, Reckitt, PensionBee, Ruggable, Haleon and Specsavers.

Previously, Tom held senior positions at design, creative and social agencies. Before that, he was a failed musician, chef and comedian.

Tom is also the host of the podcasts *Shiny New Object* and *Advertisers Watching Ads*, which explore the world of advertising and marketing with industry leaders.

LinkedIn: www.linkedin.com/in/tomollerton

FOREWORD

My fascination with the power of data began in the late 1990s, before the commercial years of the internet. I was working in marketing for a big automotive brand, and we spent a ton of money on sponsorships and media. However, the process of spending large amounts of money and waiting six months to see what sales were like became unsatisfying. That all changed when I was asked to take on a stretch assignment and think about how this company should engage with the internet.

As consumers began to engage with brands online, I became driven by curiosity about what the trail of data could reveal – like breadcrumbs leading to insight that could be used for creative, or the product, or the experience... it was in this moment that I had a pivotal 'aha' realization: the internet isn't the important part; the data behind it is. That changed everything for me.

When Tom Ollerton invited me to write the foreword for this book I couldn't have been more honoured. Looking back, I know my younger self would have benefited from having this 'compass' to help navigate the complexities of data-informed creativity and craft smarter strategies with far less guesswork.

The evolution of the craft

There are few forces reshaping the marketing industry as quickly as the evolution of data-driven strategies and their profound impact on the creative process. I've seen this transformation first-hand throughout my career, working with iconic brands like Disney, Viacom and Under Armour. Along the way, I've learned some tough lessons about creative execution – namely, that even the most well-crafted strategies and sharpest instincts can fall short without the precision and insights that data provides.

Wanting to learn as much as I could about this new channel and how it could be used to shape consumer interactions, I left the familiar and comfortable world of the multinational corporation behind to jump into the nascent world of online brokerages. Facing the challenges of building trust in investing in this new channel, creating enough engaging content around stocks and mutual funds, and a limited marketing budget, I was forced to test all our creative hypotheses. The real breakthrough for me was marrying both behaviour and demographic data in our content and offerings. This led to the creation of personalized newsletters, partnerships and the first forum for investors online, essentially an early version of Reddit that focused on stocks.

Data and storytelling: a powerful combination

During my time at Disney, I witnessed the ultimate example of how the marriage of storytelling and data analytics has transformed the customer experience. We used data to understand guests' preferences and behaviour, leading to personalization of experiences before, during and after their visit to the theme park.

The rapid growth of online channels, each with diverse formats requiring tailored content, has made it crucial to adopt smarter strategies for effectively reaching and engaging consumers. It was during a more recent role, as I was looking for ways to scale bespoke content, that I was first introduced to Tom, founder of Automated Creative.

Modernizing a legacy brand with data-driven creativity

In 2021, I joined Bose as its first-ever Chief Marketing Officer with the goal of modernizing the brand, engaging new audiences and driving growth after a challenging decade. The pressure was high, but so was the potential. Even before the pandemic, consumer purchasing behaviours were shifting dramatically, and in an increasingly crowded market, consumers were seeking more immersive, personalized content – content that went beyond a simple list of product specifications.

Bose is a brand built on 60 years of sound experience. As a company for music fans, by music fans, the data showed that collaborating with emerging artists was the right path to demonstrate a passion shared by music lovers everywhere. This allowed Bose to show what it represents rather than just telling people, building far greater trust in that creative content. By intertwining music into cultural moments like the NBA, fashion weeks or the Grammys, it showed the world just how culturally relevant the brand is today.

Building personalized content at scale was a massive undertaking – requiring significant investment, resources and risk – but it was a necessary shift from traditional product-led marketing that Bose had known previously and an investment in a new way of marketing.

The blend of data and creativity refined our storytelling, ensuring that our messages resonated and reached audiences at the right moments and could be refined in real-time to optimize their effectiveness. This is when creativity and data truly work together: when the message is on-point and resonates deeply with the audience.

The power of partnership

Creativity will always be my first passion, but when paired with data, it's like a dance – both are essential to creating something truly magical. While storytelling is where my heart lies, Tom and I have a bit of a difference: he's all about data, through and through. But that's what makes our partnership so powerful – his data-driven approach helps refine and sharpen my creative instincts, making that magic even stronger.

Automated Creative's approach allowed us to continuously refine that creative process. We worked side by side with data and analytics teams to define success and establish clear parameters. Then, we handed the brief to external creators, giving them the freedom to craft the content without predefined scripts. The results? When this model works, everyone internalizes it as the new way forward.

A guide for the data-driven age

Using Creativity and Data in Marketing is an indispensable guide for anyone looking to modernize their marketing approach or refine existing strategies. This book offers invaluable insights into navigating the ever-evolving intersection of data and creativity, helping you unlock the full potential of both. By applying these insights, you can not only enhance the effectiveness of your marketing efforts but also drive meaningful transformations in your business, creating greater value for both you and your customers.

Tom's book will challenge your assumptions, spark fresh ideas and inspire you to take calculated risks. The unique blend of creativity, data and agility outlined within is the key to making a lasting impact and maximizing the return on your marketing investments. Whether you're looking to refine your current approach or revolutionize your strategy, this book provides the tools you need to thrive in the data-driven marketing era.

Jim Mollica
President, Luxury Consumer Audio & Chief Marketing Officer, Bose

ACKNOWLEDGEMENTS

Massive thanks to Alex Hobhouse and Rhoda Sell, my business partners at Automated Creative, for giving me the space to and support to write this book. Thanks to Amy Wright for telling me to pull my finger out and start writing. And to the whole Automated Creative team in all parts of the world who are pushing the boundaries of how data and creativity make better ads for everyone.

To Donna Goddard and the team at Kogan Page for turning a rambling Google Doc full of anecdotes into something that (hopefully) reads like a book. Thank you for your patience and encouragement.

To the dozens of marketing folk who gave up their time to be interviewed for this project, you know who you are. You challenged my assumptions, inspired the stories and made this book what it is. I'm deeply grateful.

Let's be honest, most business books don't get read to the end. But you seem to have made it this far – thank you! If you are reading this then send me an email at tom@automatedcreative.net with the title 'Pink Unicorns' and let's go for a coffee.

— Tom

LIST OF CONTRIBUTORS

If you want to understand modern marketing where data and creativity collide, you need to learn from people who've actually helped shape the way it works. The people I interviewed have tested their theories on real campaigns, made real mistakes, sparked real change and still want to learn more.

The contributors to this book are those kinds of people.

Some are professors who've shaped the way the industry thinks. Others are founders who've built companies to solve problems they couldn't ignore. There are the disruptors, the deep thinkers, the technologists, the analysts, the creatives, the cynics, the optimists and the people who somehow manage to be all of the above in one conversation.

Together, they represent brands you know, platforms you probably advertise on and theories you've probably disagreed with at some point. They come from tech, FMCG, academia, creative, media, consultancy, research and leadership roles across every corner of marketing. Some have MBAs. Others have stand-up comedy nights. Most have both a point of view and the data to back it up.

They don't all agree with each other. That's the point.

These are the thinkers and doers whose experiences have shaped this book, each bringing their own take on how we can use data and creativity together. Their bios follow so I encourage you to read them and you'll quickly see why their ideas carry weight.

Rory Sutherland is the Vice Chairman of Ogilvy in the UK. He was introduced to the potential of digital marketing weirdly early, since his brother's flatmate had previously shared digs with Tim Berners-Lee while at CERN. In the following 30 years, he has continued to find the various approaches developed in digital marketing a strange mixture of the ingenious and the infuriating, and regularly finds that too many babies have been discarded with the analogue bathwater. Rory also writes regularly on technology matters for *The Spectator*, *Wired* and the *Telegraph*.

Angela Culver is the Managing Director and CMO for Services Marketing at Citi, based in New York City. With a distinguished career in global B2B and B2B2C organizations, Angela has led marketing teams across Enterprise Software and SaaS/Cloud environments.

Angela has successfully collaborated with C-suite executives, sales and product teams to drive transformation and growth. Her unique approach to marketing is rooted in her deep understanding of both science and maths, which she developed early in life through her passion for figure skating. By applying mathematical principles to improve consistency in skating, she learned to minimize variables and optimize performance – a mindset she now brings to marketing.

Throughout her career, Angela has applied data-driven strategies to accelerate business growth, develop customer-focused initiatives and build high-performing teams. Her ability to blend creativity with data analytics allows her to uncover valuable insights that drive revenue and strengthen brand affinity. Angela's international experience, combined with her passion for developing talent, has enabled her to lead teams that consistently exceed business goals.

Her journey from figure skating to marketing reflects her belief in using data to leapfrog historical trends and achieve measurable success in real-time. Angela's expertise in harnessing the power of data and creativity has made her a transformational leader in marketing, focused on delivering business-critical results and fostering growth across all channels.

Neil Patel is the co-founder of NP Digital. The *Wall Street Journal* calls him a top influencer on the web, *Forbes* says he is one of the top 10 marketers, and *Entrepreneur Magazine* says he created one of the 100 most brilliant companies. Neil is a *New York Times* bestselling author and was recognized as a top 100 entrepreneur under the age of 30 by President Obama and a top 100 entrepreneur under the age of 35 by the United Nations.

Cecilia Dones ('Ceci') is a multidisciplinary expert who views data as a creative medium for storytelling and self-expression. As a data and analytics practitioner-academic, author and international speaker, she explores the intricate relationships between technology, data and human behaviour.

Drawing from her extensive experience across FMCG, financial services, telecommunications and pharmaceuticals, Ceci has architected and led digital transformation initiatives that reshape enterprise-level people, processes and platforms. She guides organizations in leveraging AI's potential while navigating ethical considerations and consumer trust.

Ceci's academic journey includes a bachelor's degree in Marketing and International Business from NYU Stern School of Business, with minors in Psychology and East Asian Studies, and a master's in Statistics from Columbia University. Her ongoing doctoral research examines interpersonal trust signals in ambiguous virtual environments.

In her teaching roles at Columbia Business School, MIT Sloan and UPenn Wharton, Ceci incorporates innovative exercises from the performing arts, encouraging learners to reflect on their perception of reality and translate it into digital signals for data analysis. This unique approach bridges the gap between creative expression and analytical rigour.

Ceci's weekly newsletter, 'Authentic Interactions', delves into the multi-faceted aspects of trust and authenticity in the digital age. Her contributions at the intersection of AI, marketing and ethics shape both academic dialogue and industry standards, illustrating that data analysis is as much about creativity and storytelling as it is about numbers.

Jagdish N. Sheth is Charles H. Kellstadt Professor of Business in the Goizueta Business School at Emory University. He is globally known for his scholarly contributions in consumer behaviour, relationship marketing, competitive strategy and geopolitical analysis. Professor Sheth has over 50 years of combined experience in teaching and research at the University of Southern California, the University of Illinois at Urbana-Champaign, Columbia University, MIT and Emory University. He is an expert on consumer behaviour, the impact of technology on society and globalization of competition. Professor Sheth has been an advisor to numerous corporations all over the world, and has authored or coauthored more than 300 papers and several books.

Tina Eskridge is a trailblazing Global Marketing and Strategy Executive, renowned for seamlessly merging creativity with data analytics to drive groundbreaking solutions. Most recently, as the Head of Digital Marketing for Microsoft Advertising, she revolutionized the growth marketing and digital transformation strategy function for Microsoft's $12.2 billion ads business. Under her leadership, her team harnessed innovative insights and cutting-edge data to fuel growth across 14 geographical markets, spanning the Americas, EMEA and APAC.

Before this, Tina's creative vision reimagined Microsoft's inclusion marketing and product strategy across all cloud platforms. In her role leading the channel operations organization in North and Latin America, she optimized device sales and operations for top retailers such as Amazon, Best Buy, Walmart, Target, GameStop and Costco. Additionally, she drove the Global Partner and Channel Marketing GTM strategy for Microsoft's Internet of Things (IoT) business. Prior to Microsoft, Tina's passion for innovation thrived in diverse industries including retail, finance, software, consumer goods and education. Tina currently leverages her experience in both multinational corporations and PE-backed firms to bring both physical and digital products to market with unparalleled skill, serving as Managing Director and CEO of Hackrobat, LLC.

Beyond her corporate achievements, Tina actively advises and engages in early-stage VC investments. She's a seasoned non-profit board leader and an unwavering advocate for diversity, equity and inclusion. Holding dual B.S. degrees in marketing and supply chain management from Syracuse University and an MBA from Howard University, Tina currently resides in Brooklyn, NY.

Amitava Chattopadhyay is the GlaxoSmithKline Chaired Professor of Corporate Innovation at INSEAD. He is an expert on branding and innovation, and his research on these topics has appeared in leading international journals. He has published an award-winning book entitled *The New Emerging Market Multinationals: Four strategies for disrupting markets and building brands*. He has been a member of the Board of the Association for Consumer Research and is a Fellow of the Nanyang Centre for Emerging Markets. Aside from teaching in degree programmes, Professor Chattopadhyay has taught in senior management programmes in Europe, the Americas, Asia, Australia and Africa. He is a consultant to multinational firms and holds a PhD in business from the University of Florida.

Tash Beecher is a Creative Director with a viewpoint grounded in a deep love and respect for science, data and tech. After founding the science and technology section of the University of Nottingham's *Impact* magazine, she pivoted from a degree in pharmaceutical science to the creative communications industry, where she has stayed for 20 years as a writer, editor, radio presenter, model and marketeer. Tash is noted for her channel-agnostic tenacity to drive intersectional industry change – in her award-winning creative work at the best healthcare advertising agencies in the world, as a judge at global awards and as a creative leader.

Hakan Yurdakul is the founder and CEO of Bolt Insight, an AI-powered conversational research company revolutionizing insights. With 20 years in marketing – mostly at Unilever, leading global categories and brands – he understands the intersection of creativity, data and strategy. Transitioning into the entrepreneurial world, Hakan is on a mission to transform how brands uncover insights. His vision: the AI Assistant Chief Insights Officer, a real-time intelligence hub that integrates existing company data and autonomously conducts new research to fill gaps. By merging AI with human expertise, he's shaping the future of data-driven marketing and innovation.

With nearly a 20-year marketing track record at Unilever across geographies and categories, **Sinem Kaynak** is currently leading the company's Personal Care Breakthrough Innovation Group, responsible for new brand acquisitions and launches. She has previously held the Chief Growth Officer role at Unilever's Elida Beauty business unit, responsible for the unit's marketing strategy, advertising model and agency management. A champion of marketing effectiveness and efficiency, Sinem has been building new ROI monitoring models and measurement strategies in the ever-evolving marketing landscape.

Tom Goodwin is the four time #1 in 'Voice in Marketing' on LinkedIn, with over 735,000 followers on the platform. He currently heads up 'All We Have Is Now', a digital business transformation consultancy designed to unleash the power of new technology to help businesses improve.

Tom enjoys combining the world of speaking, writing and punditry with practical advisory work with clients. He's the host of *The Edge*, a TV series focusing on technology and innovation, and a podcast called 'My Wildest Prediction', both produced and distributed by Euronews.

In 2021 Tom published the second edition of his book *Digital Darwinism* with Kogan Page, and in 2023 launched a comprehensive online Digital Transformation course. He has now spoken in over 100 cities in 45 countries around the world.

With a 23-year career that spans creative, PR, digital and media agencies and also launching his own (failed) consulting business, Tom is an industry provocateur as a columnist for the *Guardian*, *TechCrunch* and *Forbes* and frequent contributor to *GQ*, The World Economic Forum, *Ad Age*, *Wired*, *Ad Week*, *Inc*, *MediaPost* and *Digiday*.

Tom was a founding member of Wharton's Future of Advertising Board, and runs a global inspiration event and podcast called 'Interesting people in interesting times', which has featured Andrew Yang, Scott Galloway and Jaron Lanier. Tom is based in Miami and London.

Lucy Jameson founded Uncommon Creative Studio in 2017. Uncommon is dedicated to building brands that people in the real world are glad exist. Uncommon has grown from three people to 300 people, with offices in London, NYC and Stockholm. They are *Ad Age*'s International Agency of the Year, a Contagious Pioneer and *Fast Company*'s #1 Innovative Company in Marketing and Advertising.

Lucy works with clients such as British Airways, ITV, Google, Ocado and PepsiCo's Quaker, along with a range of challengers and sustainable brands across brand strategy, design, advertising and CX. Uncommon has also invested in three feature films and an impact-led accelerator for start-ups, Unrest, which aims to close the funding gap for women and minorities.

Peter Field spent 15 years as a strategic planner in advertising and has been a marketing consultant for the last 25 years. Effectiveness case study analysis underpins much of his work, which includes a number of well-known texts in partnership with Les Binet, such as *The Long & The Short of It*, *Effectiveness in Context* and *The 5 Principles of Growth in B2B Marketing*. In 2024 he helped kickstart the 'cost of dull' project to alert marketers to the downsides of dull creative and media choices. Peter has a global reputation as an effectiveness expert and speaks and consults on this topic regularly around the world.

Barbara Galiza is a growth and marketing analytics consultant based in Amsterdam. She's the founder of 021 Newsletter, where she shares actionable strategies on marketing data and analytics, empowering marketers to leverage data effectively.

Over the years, Barbara has partnered with leading companies like Microsoft, WeTransfer, Veed, dbt Labs and top marketing agencies like Dentsu and Phiture, supporting them in developing growth models, implementing advanced analytics and optimizing digital campaigns.

She began her career in Brazil and moved to London in 2013, joining Y Combinator-backed HER as an early team member. Since 2017, Barbara has worked independently, helping tech brands make better marketing decisions with data.

Matt Cosad has spent the past decade helping big brands like Dove, Heinz and Comcast evolve their approach to digital marketing through technology, data and organizational change. As Head of Martech and AI for Kraft Heinz International he is leading the in-housing of tools, talent and technology to increase data fluency in the business and innovate in creative production.

Rosie Yakob is the co-founder of the nomadic consultancy Genius Steals. She blends data-driven insights with creative disruption for agencies and brands around the world. Since 2013, she's travelled to 55+ countries, developing non-traditional ways to solve business problems. Her work – recognized by Cannes, CLIO, Effies and Addy – demonstrates how analytics and creativity forge powerful brand narratives. A thought leader published in *Fast Company*, *WARC* and *Digiday*, Rosie helps organizations ignite innovation from within. She's shaped industry standards while continuously challenging conventional wisdom. Rosie is a self-proclaimed advertising enthusiast with a soft spot for curiosity, good ideas, long walks and yoga.

With The Liberty Guild, **Jon Williams** has built 'a creative business for our new world'. With a leading DE&I profile and a B Corp certification, the 500+ strong global network of A-list talent is redefining the way creativity is bought and sold. In a past life, as Chief Creative Officer of Grey EMEA, he was the first digital native to run a legacy creative department. He transformed its creative output to deliver more Lions than any other region, in the then Ad Age Global Network Agency of the Year. Jon has been foreman of, or sat on, pretty much every creative jury there is.

Meredith Herman is VP, Head of Global Marketing Acceleration at Kenvue. Prior to that role she spent over 10 years leading Global Marketing Services at Haleon.

Meredith leads teams of marketing specialists that deliver scaled services and capabilities to power marketing transformation. Departments include Global Media, Global Marketing Operations and Production, Design, Strategic Partnerships and Healthcare Professional Experiences.

Under Meredith's leadership, she has built an in-house creative and production model, increased media sales contribution and transformed end-to-end marketing to be data-driven in pursuit of marketing effectiveness. Gartner awarded Haleon '2024 Best Use of Marketing and Communication Technology' for their use of AI and automation to deliver exceptional creative effectiveness and efficiency.

Meredith has embedded DEI and accessible practices to unlock growth with 2x minority-owned media, diversity of talent in front and behind the camera, and inclusive design from AA web standards to product innovation testing to creative measurement.

Before working in consumer healthcare, she spent 15 years at creative agencies including BBDO, Ogilvy and R/GA learning how to build brands and nurture creativity for some of the world's most iconic businesses including American Express, Unilever, TD Ameritrade and Verizon. She is a passionate advocate for diversity and inclusion and is a member of the Institute for Real Growth, as well as the ANA and MMA.

Aaron Howe oversees creative for VaynerMedia Los Angeles. As the office's Executive Creative Director, he works with clients from Visa to Brita, Tinder to Meta, and others to create impactful strategic work from tweets to Super Bowl ads – and everything in between.

Previously, Howe was Executive Creative Director at Wunderman Thompson, where he oversaw integrated and social media for Microsoft, AT&T, Acura and more. Prior to joining Wunderman Thompson, Howe worked at 72andSunny and Deutsch. He began his career as a designer at *Rolling Stone*. Aaron's work has been recognized at Cannes Lions, the One Show and the Webby Awards.

Perla Bloom is a strategy leader whose expertise sits at the intersection of creativity, data and marketing. She thrives on crafting innovative, culturally relevant brand experiences that drive measurable results. Currently leading communications planning for content, editorial and entertainment at Expedia Group, Perla previously shaped global marketing strategies for iconic EA Games franchises such as *Battlefield, The Sims* and *Need for Speed*.

Her diverse expertise spans sectors including FMCG, fintech and luxury, consistently delivering fully integrated, multi-channel campaigns. Known for her forward-thinking approach, she leverages emerging technologies like AI to create dynamic, multi-touchpoint experiences that resonate with modern audiences. Perla's commitment to creativity and innovation is matched by her ability to align brand strategies with cultural trends and audience insights.

As the host of 'Think Twice', a globally recognized podcast on entertainment marketing, she shares cutting-edge perspectives on the evolving relationship between entertainment, technology and culture. She's also a sought-after international speaker, frequently appearing at industry events and on leading podcasts.

Throughout her career, Perla has demonstrated an unwavering passion for solving complex challenges through creative storytelling and data-driven strategies. Whether leading global campaigns or engaging audiences with thought leadership, she is dedicated to pushing boundaries, driving innovation and delivering impactful results that connect brands to the cultural zeitgeist.

Tom Grogan is the Chief Transformation Officer of Mourant. He helps businesses grow by using digital tools to improve how they work. Tom's work has spanned the legal sector as well as a focusing on industries like media and entertainment, creating custom software to solve problems and find opportunities. With a mix of business, engineering and legal expertise, Tom helps companies adapt to the digital world while managing risks.

Tom is focused on unlocking value from data and technology, including AI and machine learning systems. He cuts through the pretence and hype to achieve commercial results and outcomes, underpinned by his unusual blend of knowledge across technical, legal and commercial domains.

Jess Burley is a recognized leader in digital marketing and data-driven business transformation. As Global CEO and subsequently Exec Chair of M/SIX & Partners, she spearheaded the agency's growth to a $1.8 billion global operation, expanding its footprint to 43 countries and establishing its reputation for cutting-edge digital strategies, including award-winning social media campaigns and performance marketing. Her leadership prioritized digital and data analytics, developing best-in-class capabilities in tech stack consultancy and MarTech solutions for clients like Toyota, Electronic Arts, TalkTalk Telecom PLC and Virgin Bank Plc.

Beyond agency leadership, Burley's non-executive director roles at TalkTalk Telecom PLC, Quarto PLC and UK Mail PLC provided crucial experience in navigating digital transformation within the telecoms, publishing and logistics sectors, respectively. Her work with The Mix charity further demonstrates her commitment to leveraging digital platforms for positive social impact. This effort is continued today with her role as a Trustee for the Follicular Lymphoma Foundation, whose mission is to connect oncologists across the globe, via a patient bio bank, to accelerate the discovery of a cure for Follicular Lymphoma.

Currently, as a partner at T&Pm and Future Technology Chair, Burley focuses on the intersection of AI and marketing. She empowers clients and agency teams to harness AI across the marketing mix, from data capture and audience building to creative strategy and optimized customer journeys. Her expertise lies in identifying and implementing emerging technologies to drive innovation and deliver best-in-class marketing performance.

Faris Yakob is an award winning (and losing) author, strategist, creative director and public speaker. His book *Paid Attention: Innovative advertising for a digital world* (now in second edition from Kogan Page) has been translated into multiple languages and pioneered attention-based thinking in the industry.

Alongside his wife Rosie, he is the co-founder of the creative consultancy Genius Steals, built on the belief that ideas are new combinations and nothing comes from nothing. They have travelled to more than 60 countries since 2013 giving talks and consulting with clients. They have worked with brands like Coca-Cola, agencies like OMD, Ogilvy, IPG and Accenture, media companies like Meta and trade bodies like Thinkbox, IAB and ARF on brand and business strategy, ideas, inspiration, innovation, thought leadership, workshops and training.

Faris spent five years in New York as Chief Innovation Officer (MDC Partners) and Chief Digital Officer (McCann Erickson). Formerly a management consultant, he moved into advertising and was an early employee of Naked Communications in London, moving to the Sydney and then New York offices. He has won and judged numerous awards including the Effies, Clios, One Show and LIAs. He consulted on and featured in *The Greatest Movie Ever Sold*.

The newsletter 'Strands of (Stolen) Genius' is one of the '7 essential reads for curious creatives' (HubSpot) and one of the top resources for strategists (Planning Survey). Go to http://geniussteals.co/subscribe for brief bursts of inspiration in your inbox.

Faris writes a monthly column on brand communication for the World Advertising Research Council (WARC). Bylines include the *Guardian*, the *Financial Times* and Medicat. He received his MA in English (Oxford) and won the President's Prize for his thesis for the IPA's 'Excellence Diploma in Brands'. He hopes this self-aggrandizing screed wasn't too obnoxious and that you have a lovely day.

Sam Gaunt is the founder of Working Media, a consultancy specializing in media strategy, testing and measurement. With over 20 years of experience, Sam has partnered with leading brands, including McDonald's, Haleon, Lidl and Sky, to make their marketing investments work harder and drive measurable business outcomes. His approach balances data-driven insights with a creative understanding of how media and brand assets drive demand and deliver lasting impact.

By ensuring insights are grounded in actual customer behaviour rather than relying on proxy metrics, Sam empowers marketing and finance teams to make better decisions on their marketing investment. Through Working Media, he collaborates closely with clients to build tailored measurement frameworks, design testing roadmaps and implement analytics capabilities that drive sales and build brand equity.

Lisa Calvino is Head of Digital Marketing, Brompton Bicycles Ltd. Lisa has over 13 years of digital marketing experience in the retail industry. Specializing in eCommerce, she has consistently demonstrated a strong ability to blend creativity with data-driven strategies, creating impactful campaigns that drive growth and deliver exceptional results.

Lisa excels in building and leading teams that are not only focused on performance but also rooted in collaboration, enthusiasm and a shared vision for success. Her calm and compassionate approach fosters an environment where creativity thrives, and her deep understanding of customer behaviour allows her to craft personalized marketing solutions that resonate with audiences across international markets.

In addition to her marketing expertise, Lisa is an EMCC-accredited coach, further enhancing her leadership style. Her coaching experience empowers her to inspire, mentor and develop high-performing teams, creating a culture of growth, resilience and continuous improvement.

Lisa has a proven track record of identifying untapped growth opportunities and implementing strategies that increase customer acquisition, retention and revenue generation. Her expertise spans performance marketing, data-driven customer acquisition and financial forecasting. With proficiency in SEO, PPC, affiliates, paid social and display advertising, she has helped brands exceed their financial goals through targeted, innovative campaigns that deliver measurable results.

With a unique blend of creative intuition, analytical precision and coaching skills, Lisa brings a strategic, results-oriented approach to every project. Passionate about leveraging data to drive marketing success and empowering teams, she invites you to connect, collaborate and explore how creative digital marketing can take your brand to new heights.

Adam Wright is a growth marketing leader and current Director of Growth Marketing at Sampl, a digital sampling company that uses data-driven insights to connect brands with consumers in impactful ways. Formerly Head of Digital at NIVEA, Adam has spent his career testing and scaling growth marketing teams with a focus on rapid experimentation.

Beyond his work with established brands, Adam has also applied his growth marketing and experimentation approaches to scale up DTC brands and continues to take on advisory roles, sharing his insights to accelerate growth in emerging companies.

At Sampl, Adam leads initiatives that place first-party data at the core of brand campaigns, balancing data with creativity to build campaigns that are impactful and trackable. His work enables brands to make informed decisions that drive customer acquisition and optimize retention.

Adam also shares his thoughts in a growth marketing newsletter and on LinkedIn, where he writes about the intersection of creativity, data and digital innovation. With his background spanning both corporate and scale-up environments, Adam offers a grounded, strategic perspective on modern marketing. Connect with him on LinkedIn to explore insights on data-driven growth and marketing innovation.

Becky McOwen-Banks is an AI-energized Executive Creative Director with over 20 years of experience transforming and enabling global and local teams in advertising and tech. She has led award-winning creative departments, delivering impactful campaigns for brands like UEFA Women, BMW, NIVEA, NS&I and The Girl Effect. Becky has held leadership roles at Meta, VaynerMedia London and FCB Inferno. As the founder of Plain:ai, she consults on integrating AI into creative processes, preparing teams for AI acceleration. Becky is passionate about blending data insights with imaginative thinking to craft compelling narratives that connect.

Jim Sterne is widely recognized as the Godfather of Digital Analytics, with over four decades of experience in digital marketing. His key achievements include authorship of 12 books on marketing, analytics, and AI. Education: instructor of half a dozen courses on AI and machine learning on LinkedIn Learning. Innovation: founded the Marketing Analytics Summit (2002) and the Digital Analytics Association (2004). Thought leadership: pioneered 'Marketing on the Internet' concepts since the early 1990s. Mentorship: created the Analytics Cohorts mutual mentorship programme (2021). Consulting: advises marketing departments and entrepreneurs on applying technology to marketing and enterprises on generative AI adoption. Speaking: international keynote speaker on digital media's value in customer relationships. Throughout his career, Jim has helped professionals navigate technological shifts in marketing: 1980s: computers for marketing, 1990s: marketing on the internet, 2000s: marketing analytics, 2010s: artificial intelligence for marketing, 2020s: adopting generative AI capabilities. International analytics and AI expert Jim Sterne has enlightened thousands with his clear, thoughtful and informative presentations that are tailored to each particular audience. Sterne's presentations are described as well-researched, information rich and high energy. His relevant and impactful talks are abundantly illustrated for clarity rather than decoration.

Anastasia Leng is the Founder and CEO of CreativeX, a technology company that powers creative decision making for the world's best brands. CreativeX technology is used by Fortune 500 brands like Unilever, Mondelez, Heineken, Google and more to measure creative efficiency, consistency and impact across all image and video content worldwide. Credited by the CEO of Diageo with a 50 per cent reduction to CPM and attributed by the CMO of Nestlé to a 66 per cent increase in digital ad effectiveness, today CreativeX is responsible for enabling creative measurement at scale for the world's most sophisticated brands.

Prior to CreativeX, Anastasia co-founded Hatch, one of *Time Magazine*'s Top 10 Startups to Watch in New York and one of four most innovative retail companies. Prior to Hatch, she spent 5+ years at Google, where she worked on every ad tech and analytics product, led entrepreneurship efforts in EMEA and was responsible for early-stage partnerships for Google Voice, Chrome and Wallet.

Anastasia graduated from the University of Pennsylvania with a triple major in Psychology, Sociology and French. She's been a nomad all her life and has lived in Bahrain, Vietnam, Hungary, Russia, France, England and the United States. She remains a mediocre tennis player and an aspiring writer.

Lex Bradshaw-Zanger is Chief Marketing and Digital Officer, L'Oréal South Asia Pacific, Middle East and North Africa Region (SAPMENA). Lex's career has spanned the growth of the web from the 56k modem to 5G mobile, and has covered North America, Europe, the Middle East and Asia Pacific. Prior to his current role, Lex was the CMO for the UK and Ireland, held roles in the Western Europe Zone and was Chief Digital Officer for the L'Oréal Middle East and Africa Region.

The CDMO team in the SAPMENA region has a broad reach covering deep expertise in media, data and technology as well as consumer and market intelligence – and the key responsibility today of accelerating the transformation of the eCommerce business and continuing to remain the leaders in marketing innovation. Prior to L'Oréal, Lex was with McDonald's and Facebook. He is a recovered ad man, having spent over 10 years in the agency world, with both WPP and Publicis – his last role was Regional Director for Digital Strategy and Innovation for Leo Burnett MENA.

Alongside his day job, Lex is a board member of the Mobile Marketing Association for EMEA and the Oxford Saïd Future of Marketing Initiative, and a Fellow of the Marketing Academy and the Chartered Institute of Marketing. He is also committed to giving back and using his skills for good, as an adviser to multiple start-ups and as part of the School of Marketing mentoring programme. Father of three girls, he is a #DigitalNative, Global #geek and a #Parisian. He balances time between work, the web and family – almost always on his phone.

Tiffany Rolfe is the Chair and Chief Creative Officer of R/GA, a global innovation company at the intersection of storytelling, design and technology. She leads groundbreaking work for clients like Nike, Google and Verizon, with recent highlights including Reddit's five-second Super Bowl hack, Nike Sync's menstrual cycle training app and Verizon's virtual stadium in Fortnite.

Previously, Tiffany was Partner and CCO at Co:Collective, where she launched YouTube's first creator campaigns and led MoMA's rebrand. She began her career designing websites for Pixar and Disney before joining Crispin Porter + Bogusky, where she helped shape the agency's 'Decade of Dominance' with award-winning work for MINI Cooper, American Express OPEN and the Truth anti-smoking initiative.

A visionary creative leader, Tiffany has earned top accolades from Cannes Lions, D&AD and The One Show. She is a passionate advocate for diversity and industry evolution, serving as a sought-after speaker, juror and board member for the Ad Council, the One Club and the Ad Club of NY.

Seenapse's founder and CEO, **Rafa Jiménez**, has always been captivated by technology's potential to enhance creativity. Originating from his teenage passion for music, where sequencers and synthesizers enabled him to express his ideas despite not mastering instruments, Rafa's fascination evolved with desktop publishing, interactive media and the web, which opened new avenues of expression and the chance to make a living out of creating stuff with computers.

Rafa's journey in advertising began after his digital agency was acquired by Ogilvy. It was there that he noticed how technology could transform not just production but the ideation process itself. The idea for Seenapse took root from observing search engines' limitations in uncovering unique concepts, and also from seeing how advertising creatives are very self-referential and need to break out of their bubbles.

Initially envisioned as a cultural reference search engine, Seenapse struggled with abstraction and Rafa couldn't find a way to make it more useful for people. The tech just wasn't there, and he believed machines couldn't be creative until 2016, when AlphaGo's unprecedented move convinced him otherwise. This Saint-Paul-on-the-road-to-Damascus moment led to integrating deep learning and language models with Seenapse's divergence engine, making this model truly creative.

Today, Rafa still enjoys music (but now is learning to play an instrument), shares his life between Mexico City and Bilbao with his wife (also his co-founder), and is a father to a daughter and a son.

David Byrne is Head of Brand and Marketing, with extensive experience growing brands on both sides of the agency/client axis for Leo Burnett, large blue-chip companies (Aviva/HSBC/BBC/adidas/McDonald's, IKEA, BT), scale-ups (Wealthify/Green Flag) and start-ups (67 Pall Mall/the Utopian Hotel Collection) across sectors, digital, social and analogue media in the UK, Europe and the United States. A weather maker not a fence-sitter. Apparently.

Former International Development Director at PHD, **Rupert Slade** worked in London in media from the late 1980s for CIA media network before moving to Poland in 1998. He has worked in Ireland and his last full-time job was running the PHD media network across Eastern Europe and Russia. After that he was a pitch consultant working across Europe. He has worked on pitches and won in almost every country in Europe, He became fascinated by advertising effectiveness through working with the likes of Unilever and Diageo especially, who had an abundance of data. Eastern Europe in the late 1990s was a pioneering place where almost anything felt possible. Media is a very data-heavy business but most data is used retrospectively to justify expenditure. However, the best solutions come when insight changes a whole strategy – one small insight can change everything.

Rupert loves creativity in media. He has won international and local awards. Now retired, in his late 50s he is having a serious go at being a stand-up comedian. He runs a comedy brand called Hot Paprika Comedy in Hungary.

Simon Kemp helps the world make sense of what people are really doing online. His acclaimed Global Digital Reports series has been viewed more than 100 million times by people in every country on Earth, and has become an essential resource for CEOs, CMOs, journalists, NGOs and even world leaders. Simon is the founder of Kepios, a management intelligence service, and chief analyst at DataReportal. He also advises and collaborates with a number of the world's most progressive marketing services organizations. Over the past 20 years, Simon has helped to define brand and marketing strategies for many of the world's most admired companies, including Google, Unilever, Nestlé, Coca-Cola and Diageo, and he continues to advise the world's top marketers and investors on the latest trends in digital behaviour. In addition to his research and consulting work, Simon also delivers regular guest lectures for leading academic institutions around the world. Outside of work, Simon is an electronic music nerd, and he also runs the Singapore Whisky Society. You can find him across most of the internet as 'eskimon'.

Alex Jenkins is Editorial Director at Contagious, tasked with helping brands and advertising agencies around the world understand and adapt to shifts in marketing, consumer culture and technology. Alex is responsible for the Contagious IQ intelligence platform and all content at Contagious events. Alex came to Contagious from the knowledge department of the IPA, and prior to that worked as a business journalist and copywriter.

And last and by no means least:

Jim Mollica, President, Luxury Consumer Audio and Chief Marketing Officer, joined Bose in 2021 as the company's first global chief marketing officer. He oversees the brand's strategic and creative direction, as well as its connection to consumers across all platforms and touch points. Jim specializes in digital transformation and storytelling, drawing on more than 25 years of marketing, media, digital commerce and revenue-generation expertise. He also now serves as President of the company's luxury consumer audio business, which includes McIntosh and Sonus faber. Prior to joining Bose, Jim held senior executive roles for some of the world's top consumer, lifestyle, entertainment and automotive brands, including Under Armour, Viacom/MTV Networks, The Walt Disney Company, Ralph Lauren and Nissan Motor Corporation. Jim is a graduate of the University of Pittsburgh, earning an MBA from the Katz Graduate School of Business.

Introduction

I wanted to call this book *Data vs Creativity: The battle for advertising's soul*. I thought it was punchy, provocative, something that would sit nicely in airport bookshops between *Thinking, Fast and Slow* and *Harry Potter*. But my publisher said no.

Not because it was inaccurate. But because it wouldn't work well with SEO. The title needed to contain keywords that potential buyers would type into search engines. The title that I thought was clever and creative would be undiscoverable by the audience it was intended for. My mistake here was not to use data and creativity together. Ironically, given the content of this book, I ignored the data and relied on my intuition and feel. There's nothing wrong with this approach, it's just that it's wrong more often than it's right.

I've spent my career bouncing between creative and data-driven marketing roles. At creative and digital agencies, I saw firsthand how resistant the industry could be to numbers, analysis and feedback loops that could actually improve the work. In the last eight years I've run Automated Creative with Alex Hobhouse and Rhoda Sell, and our tech has created and optimized ad creative using live data and insight. We're dedicated to the art of and science of turning every ad impression into intelligence.

So I've seen both sides and I'm fascinated by this question. How can we make better ads by using both creativity and data together?

The reality is that creativity is already shaped by data, whether we like it or not. The problem is that we're using it in the wrong way. All too often in our industry data is being used to reduce risk instead of using it to create better ideas that weren't possible before. As Tiffany Rolfe put it, 'We're using data to help us not lose. And you don't win by trying not to lose.' This book contains advice from 40 or so data-driven marketing professionals who guide you to a better way forward.

The experts interviewed for this book argue that if we see data as a rigid set of rules, then it will kill our creativity. But when used well it should be a catalyst for coming up with better ideas – the idea that marketers can stop seeing data as a box to tick and start using it to make better work.

For the first part of advertising's history, success came down to instinct. The best campaigns were the ones that won awards, shaped culture and actually sold stuff, and they were credited to brilliant minds who just knew what would work. There were no dashboards. Just a room full of ideas, a persuasive pitch and a client willing to take a leap of faith.

But in reality great ideas were never just gut feel. Even before the dawn of the dashboard, the best marketers had an unspoken understanding of their audience. They paid attention to people one way or another. They might not have called it 'data,' but they were using real world signals to spark ideas.

Fast forward to today, and we have more of those signals than we know what to do with.

Instead of unlocking new possibilities, data is being used to play it safe. Instead of making work that surprises our audiences we are using data to suffocate what is possible. That's why so much advertising today feels the same. The safest, blandest, most forgettable work isn't the result of too much data or too little creativity. It's the result of letting data do the talking and not taking a risk on creative that might actually get noticed.

This book is about changing that.

This book is for the marketers who want to prove that data doesn't replace human intuition but enhances it. If you want to make work that surprises and gets your brand noticed then this book is for you. Creativity and data are not at odds – but to make them work together, we need to change how we think about both.

So let's get started.

What you are about to read is a result of over 40 conversations with senior and experienced brand marketers, creatives, strategists, consultants, technologists, academics and industry influencers. Let's assume for the sake of argument you went for an hour-long coffee once a week with the guests in this book – that would take you about a year, and that's a lot more coffee dates than most people manage. So I've saved you a year's worth of mingling with some of the best minds in the industry to try to bring together a book that can help you combine data and creativity more effectively.

If you want access to the bonus chapters for this book and regular inspiration of data, creativity and ads then head to AutomatedCreative.net/DataAndCreativity. Or if you'd like to join the 'Marketing, Data and Creativity' WhatsApp Group, scan this code with your phone.

If you'd like to hear the full interviews with each of the brilliant minds featured throughout this book, search for the 'Shiny New Object' podcast on your platform of choice. We will be releasing them over the coming months.

Tom Ollerton
Founder
Automated Creative

01

Data demystified

I'm embarrassed to admit this, but when I started out researching for this book I thought that data meant 1s and 0s or alphanumeric data, but this is far from true. Digital data is one form of the stuff and easier to measure, but data is simply a record of something happening. This can either be beautiful, clean structured data or a chaotic soup of sensory experiences. And what makes it more interesting is that they are both exciting and useful for advertising folk. As I had conversations with senior advertising professionals, I became increasingly red faced as I realized that the world I live and work in is a small niche within a ginormous ecosystem of interconnected qualitative (qual) and quantitative (quant) data.

I started working in marketing when social media had begun to go mainstream, and that has always been my reference point. I never worked at a classic advertising agency, I never worked on a TV advert and I never won a Cannes Lion Award. It was not my world. The sunken treasure of 'below the line' is where I've been for over 17 years, so that was my starting point and the experts in this book have given me a whole new perspective. If you seek, you find, you learn and now I'm wiser and hopefully I can share some of what I've discovered in this book.

So, not all data is words and numbers; it's the soft and mushy stuff that comes out of focus groups or is overheard on buses or casually shared in a lift – this is also very much data. Or, as the academic Jagdish Sheth puts it, 'Data doesn't mean quantitative data. Data does not mean unstructured big data.'

This chapter attempts to clarify what the word 'data' actually means for marketers today beyond just numbers and spreadsheets. So, let's begin by defining data and then explore how it fuels insight, intuition and creativity.

Using data to derive insights

Data that doesn't create insight (and consequently inspire ideas for advertising purposes) is just information. Every spreadsheet, every dashboard, every PowerPoint presentation that sits silently on a server is just noise that sits waiting to waste someone's time. Data has no value other than the price someone was paid to extract that data from somewhere. At Automated Creative we believe that if data doesn't inspire an idea then it's just information.

That's not to say there's no power in piles of data. I've been involved in many pitches where an agency bod has said 'The brand needs to look more complicated' or 'Make it seem more complex than it is'. Even a high-flying consultant at a big firm said when they present to clients he says 'We need to make it look like a fifty grand deck'. So, if you want to dazzle someone who doesn't know any better with a snowstorm of data you may get a short-term win. But if the audience are any good, they will say 'so what?' And unless you can turn that data into an insight and that insight into an idea that boosts sales, you're wasting everyone's time – including your own.

Annoyingly, definitions of an insight are vast in number. Sam Gaunt says 'McDonald's wouldn't mind me mentioning their name against it but they've defined an insight as "consumer understanding that inspires brand growth"… that's really stuck with me over the years.' Data is abundant, insight is common, inspiration is in short supply and brand growth is unfortunately rarer than we would like.

Marketing at its best elicits emotion. Emotion comes from something surprising and something new, not the same old same old. In order to have something new that gets an audience emotional then we need an idea. And based on knowledge I've learned from creatives, the best chance of getting to an idea that creates an emotion is to have an insight. And insight comes from data, be it tidy numbers and letters or messy observances of people. Data can come from anywhere and take any form.

Data and intuition

There's an interesting relationship between data and intuition. You could say they are enemies. One is perceived as cold and the other perceived as magic. Data can be seen as the opposite of intuition. Data can be captured externally in a document, file, recording, spreadsheet or even mad scribblings on a serviette. This differs from our seemingly mysterious ability to draw from intuition. Intuition is how humans process data collected from the senses and synthesize it as ideas and feelings. Humans are little data processors constantly absorbing data from the world.

Without data, intuition starves. Who would be more likely to come up with a great advertising idea – someone who sits in a dark room with no contact with the real or digital world, or a curious and data-hungry character who is immersed in the world? I don't know how ideas specifically spark in the brain; that's less important for this book. What we're after is better ads. We want ads that drive real emotions, real actions and sales. In order to do this we must provide ideas fuelled with intuition derived from our own personal data.

The necessity of using data

When speaking to 'AI-energized Executive Creative Director' Becky McOwen-Banks, she dived deeper into what data is: 'The definition of data is so vast. What data means now and what data meant many years ago feels different.' Becky explains that data used to be a 'dirty word' in the marketing world because it was associated with the less glamorous end of the industry like direct mail and lower-funnel sales metrics. But that is no longer the case: 'Data is now very much top table conversation, not people in weird spaces, for those who are curious or just constantly hungry to try different things. Suddenly, it has been lifted into the light.'

Data can be many things, in many places, to many people. It doesn't fit nicely into boxes and its unruly nature can be a problem for marketers. It also provides an opportunity for marketers to make work that matters. Another option is to guess and make it up – which is in fact your brain processing external data in the form of intuition and ideas. So, however you go about it, you're using data. It's not a choice of whether you use data or not, it's a choice of how good you want to be.

According to Tiffany Rolfe, there are different buckets of data:

- **Cultural:** This data looks at what's happening in the world, culture and people. It particularly gives insight into human behaviour.
- **Persona:** This focuses on second- and third-party data, specifically location, demographics, certain affinities and behaviours. In order to create customized experiences, you need this kind of data.

- **Behavioural:** This data is based on the customer interaction with an experience. Where are they clicking? How are they using something? This is where you can help create more personalized messages and experiences based on how customers interact with a product.
- **User actions:** Based on owned properties such as a website, app or physical location, this data creates more valuable services.

Rolfe's view is that cultural data and persona data are mostly used in advertising, while behavioural data and user data feed more into RGA's 'product' and 'experience' work. These definitions of data are useful as they give you a few buckets to go and look in to see how full they are. The huge mass of data that rains down on marketers is easier to make sense of when you start to group them together and label them. It's about having the right data for the right job.

Seeing the big picture of data

The important lesson for marketers is to not get too obsessed with the data that's easy to get your hands on. You may own a certain data set but it's only going to be part of the whole picture. Perla Bloom advises:

> It's important to understand the shortcomings of both kinds of data. Qualitative self-reports aren't always reliable because what people think they do and want is not always what they actually do. And it's not plain sailing with qualitative data. It doesn't tell the whole story; you might be seeing a correlation versus causation.

Tom Goodwin's view is:

> I am a passionate believer in qual. Quant has a time and a place, but qual as a way to inform the process is extraordinary. I'm sure you end up in conversations about semantics but the degree to which someone is telling you their ideas from a call session, or their frustrations when checking into your hotel – you could say they are conversations around data.

Data is many things from many places; quant and qual are a square peg and a round hole. It's your job as a marketer to not pick a side but to be open to the charms and failings of each in the pursuit of an insight that will nurture creative ideas that will help grow the brands you represent.

KEY TAKEAWAYS

- Data isn't just numbers, it's any observation or experience, digital or human.
- Intuition is your brain's own data processing system – embrace it.
- Data that doesn't inspire action is just noise.

02

From analogue to algorithms

This isn't a yawn-inducing history lesson, I promise. But if you want to know why we do the weird stuff marketers do today, you need a quick rewind through marketing's greatest hits. Let's quickly look at how data and marketing have always gone hand in hand.

It's a cold day in winter and I'm attending an advertising event in London. It's a significant event in the marketing industry that offers brands and agencies insights into how to get more sales online. This should be the fusion of the highest levels of creativity and technology but the event by industry standards is small. Getting customers to part with their hard-earned cash online isn't new but this event doesn't feel like an exploding part of the industry. It's populated with tech vendors talking about data lead technical products. There are no creative agencies sponsoring or the usual tropes of creative talent or a sense of excitement. It feels like an event where control is all powerful, a church of the 1s and 0s. This event seems intent on locking things down, squeezing an extra drop of juice out of a brand's media spend. This event fails to synthesize exciting tech with creativity. It feels like data has won the battle for the bottom of the funnel with dark and silent whirring automation. While data provides much-needed rigour, true creativity continues to defy rigid frameworks. This book is about the idea that data and creativity are better with each other and not confined to different ends of the playground. Consumers, brands and agencies deserve better.

But before we get to that, let's go back in time to London in 1477.

The oldest surviving advert is for a book that is a guide for priests called *Sarum Pie*. William Caxton, who was England's first commercial printer, wanted to drive footfall to his shop, and cleverly employed different ways of doing this. He marketed *Sarum Pie* by printing an ad in the same typeface as the book itself. This allowed the audience to get a sample of the product just by looking at the ad. Caxton created the ad in the same manufacturing process as the product and assured the viewer of the quality and accuracy. As well as the technical accuracy of the printing, the ad also included details about the price. Accuracy of the product and cost were important to the audience (priests at the time) but the advert also had a direct call to action telling them to visit Caxton's shop in Westminster. The ad's final clever creative tactic was to ensure it was seen by asking its viewers, 'Please do not remove this notice', suggesting that the ad was likely displayed in a church porch often used by church officials.

We've seen the modern techniques of direct response, sampling, price, call to action, customer centricity and viewability all crammed into an ancient ad that attempts to collapse the marketing funnel by making priests aware of the new product and driving them to purchase.[1] We'll have to guess if Caxton kept any data on whether sales improved but given there may have been very few ads to compete with, it may have had good ROI.

A brief history of data in marketing

We're going to fast-forward to the dawn of marketing and see how the use of data has changed as technology has evolved. Let's begin in the late 19th century, when mass production and branded goods became a thing, and manufacturers started paying attention to customer feedback. These weren't organized surveys, just clever business owners listening to shopkeepers and customers. Their passing comments provided valuable insights into which products sold well and why.

The foundation of data storage and advertising (1881–1950s)

1881 – when the US Census Bureau struggled to process vast amounts of population data, Herman Hollerith invented the Tabulating Machine. This system used punch cards to automate data processing and reduced the time required for large-scale data analysis, and his innovation later became the foundation of IBM.[2] While initially created for government use, this technology also influenced businesses, including advertisers who now had a way to process consumer data more efficiently.

1920s – everything changed when developments in psychology from early advertising visionaries introduced the idea that human decision making is driven by emotional and social triggers. Around this time, advertisers consulted psychologists to conduct personal interviews and conversations with small groups of consumers to understand what actually influenced buying behaviour. While this was happening the rise of mass media advertising through radio and print transformed the industry. Brands began to realize they could use consumer surveys and coupon redemptions to measure audience engagement, offering a first glimpse of data-driven marketing.

Advertising meets sociology (1940s–1950s)

1940s – sociologists who had studied wartime propaganda developed group interview techniques that were later adopted by advertisers. Their approach provided a structured way to get subjective consumer feedback, allowing brands to observe consumers talking about their products. Advertisers would sit behind two-way mirrors, watching with fascination as participants discussed brands and products, getting awfully excited about the insights these focus groups unearthed.

1950s – television became massive and revolutionized the ability to reach consumers with advertising, blossoming into a mass market industry. However, data collection was still limited and the only way to measure TV's effectiveness was through Nielsen ratings and broad demographic studies. Around this time advertising agencies began tapping into consumers' deeper desires through in-depth interviews inspired by psychology. Researchers paid close attention to personal stories, emotional associations, body language and tone of voice, believing these cues provided powerful insights into consumer behaviour.

The shift to digital storage and computing (1960s–1980s)

1960s – 'Mad Men'-style marketers took an even more immersive approach to marketing. Curious planners and creatives from ad agencies visited consumers in their homes to listen to stories and experiences where they lived. They created 'consumer portraits' and personas based on their observations of attitudes, language and behaviours. The introduction of mainframe computers during this era also allowed companies to store consumer data more effectively, shifting from manual tracking to computerized databases.

1970s – ad land took inspiration from anthropology and visited shops and other public settings to observe how brands' goods were used in everyday life. Marketers had a better understanding of in-store behaviours, realizing that people didn't always shop in the way they claimed to in surveys. This decade also saw the emergence of the first databases and early customer relationship management (CRM) systems, allowing brands to collect structured data on purchasing behaviours and demographics. This set the stage for direct marketing, enabling brands to refine their messaging based on past purchases.

1980s – direct marketing provided a real-world observational approach that extended to the shopping malls which were becoming an increasing consumer staple. Agencies would keep an eagle eye on how consumers behaved in these spaces, tracking what caught their attention and what led to spontaneous purchases. Researchers weren't shy about approaching shoppers in the moment, asking them what they were thinking and why they looked at a certain product. The goal was to capture insights as they happened, rather than relying on consumers to self-report later.

Meanwhile, personal computers (PCs) and spreadsheet software made data analysis more accessible to marketers. Companies could now analyse consumer trends, segment audiences and refine targeting strategies without relying on massive mainframes. Marketers also began experimenting with loyalty programmes, offering incentives in exchange for consumer data, which further refined their understanding of individual purchasing patterns. Brands were beginning to understand that not all customers were the same, and data could be used to tailor messaging more precisely.

1990s – advertising researchers embraced role-playing workshops, home visits and immersive studies. In retrospect, these efforts feel meticulous, empathetic and slightly intrusive, but they marked the last major era of human-centred consumer research before the rapid digital transformation that would change everything.

What was to come was very, very different.

The web as an advertising platform (1990s)

In the early 1990s the internet was pretty hard to use; it was mostly text used by academics and tech fans. Once the World Wide Web showed up things got interesting and being online started to become more visually interesting and easier to use. The idea that we could cram ads into one fairly accessible thing became a thing. Brands started saying, 'Give me eyeballs, I'll give you money'.

The early internet was pioneered by the military and academics so it's hard to think that the eyeball-popping internet is related to the sedate message boards of ancient digital times. But the internet had the best of intentions – social intentions, in fact.

During this decade the web was accessible only through dial-up devices; you had to use the phone line. So, if you wanted to get online you had to beat someone to the phone and if you wanted to make a call you'd have to listen to a modem screeching.

The invention of the web was in itself a combination of data and creativity. Before the web was invented the only way to access information was a pain that required specialist knowledge of commands and network addresses. Tim Berners-Lee was working at CERN, the European Organization for Nuclear Research, which was the home of lots of physicists collaborating in different locations.

Researchers needed to share and access documents using different devices, systems and formats. Sharing information was inefficient and fragmented. Berners-Lee's creative vision was to bring all the research data together and to create a space where all the researchers could share their findings easily without any faff. Berners-Lee's solution was to create clickable words in a document or a 'hypertext' to link documents. This linked data points together in a way that let the user choose their path as opposed to it being a linear process where one thing came after another. It gave the user choice, agency.

Data and creativity aren't always comfortable bedfellows. Berners-Lee's original proposal for the web was turned down and it wasn't until his second attempt that he got the go-ahead. Creativity and data often need a push.

The early days of digital marketing

HotWired was the online sibling of *Wired* magazine and was one of the first commercial web magazines to try to make money online. As it looked around for a business model, online ads became a possibility. Digital ads were mostly uncharted territory, with no rules, metrics or dashboards.

The first banner ad was for AT&T. The *HotWired* team sold them the dream of a clickable banner ad that said 'Have you ever clicked your mouse right HERE? You will.'

Not only was the ad the grandparent of all clickbait but it was also rainbow coloured. It looks a little like an army recruitment ad made by a five-year-old who loves unicorns. But the ad drove to an AT&T website that promoted art museums. This ad lacked the finesse and creativity of William Caxton's ad for *Sarum Pie* in 1477, but something new had started on 27 October, 1994.

Despite the ad's creative shortcomings it did what it set out to do – get people to click on it. In fact 44 per cent of the people who saw the ad clicked on it. No one knew what that meant other than people had clicked on the ad – no one really knew why. Ironically there are many in our industry decades later still asking, 'Someone clicked on our ad, so what?'

This ad showed that not only could you show someone an ad, but you could make them do something. Up to this point any direct correlation from an individual user to an outcome that a brand wanted was more difficult to prove. This was direct, it happened, you could prove it. Someone had a creative idea, someone made it, someone else put that ad in front of someone and someone clicked on it – and we knew how many. Brilliant, what could go wrong?

Despite this lack of transparency the likes of Volvo, Club Med, Zumba and MCI joined the online advertising display banner party bus and the industry outgrew its capacity to deliver quality work. Joe McCambley, the creator of the first banner ad, explained in an article for the *Guardian* that the internet has been flooded with advertisers and as online advertising grew the quality could not meet the demand, so quick, cheap advertising has become a priority.[3] And we all know what that looks like today.

Cookies – giving the internet a memory

Around the same time a founding engineer at Netscape, Lou Montulli, decided to try and give the internet a memory in the form of a cookie. The internet was a growing set of unconnected experiences as advertisers tried to understand their place in it. Each time a user visited a website it was like groundhog day. Each time they came back, the website had no way of realizing it was the same person again. This was particularly galling for e-commerce shops that had no way of remembering what you'd been looking at last time you visited.

Montulli took inspiration from 'magic cookies', which was a practice from computer programming where a program shares a small piece of information with another program and returns it when it is needed. It's a little like a cloakroom attendant giving you a ticket so that they know which is your coat when you come back to collect it. Montulli applied this idea to the internet and created cookies that allowed websites to remember you and what you did. This allowed the business to make the website experience better next time you visited, meaning sites could track your shopping cart, your preferences and log-in status. Giving the internet a memory solved a huge problem, but not all memories are things we want to keep. The promise of the cookie was that it would open up a more personalized and creative internet but it also delivered a new power for data-driven marketing.[4]

However, with great power comes great responsibility.

The invention of cookies kicked off a debate that continues to the time of writing around privacy and data protection, making their future seem unlikely. While cookies made the internet more user-friendly and opened up new avenues for data and creativity, they also raised concerns about how personal information was being used. The story of the invention of cookies is typical in the history of data and creativity; it was a moment where necessity inspired ingenuity, leading to a solution that changed the way we used the internet. But it also serves as a reminder of how technology can transform the way we interact with the world around us, for better and for worse.

The internet starts to make money

In 1995 the internet was still an academic tool – one might argue it was all data and no creativity. But where there's attention from consumers there's money to be made. In that year the National Science Foundation Network (NSFNET) was decommissioned, heralding the start of the commercial internet. Once the barriers were removed the number of websites went from a few hundred in 1993 to over 100,000 by the end of 1996.[5] The data started to be quite something.

From then on it went bananas, and as sites like Amazon, eBay and Yahoo took off, the venture capital money poured in to inflate an ever-growing bubble of dotcom businesses. It was a gold rush with thousands of folk eager to get rich on internet gold. The interesting change in consumer behaviour at this time was the fact that people would pay for things online – eBay and Amazon made sure of that.

Amazon was an online bookshop originally, but Jeff Bezos had his sights on bigger things. Amazon pioneered the use of data and analytics to personalize recommendations for online shopping. Amazon's use of data analytics to give personalized recommendations is an important story in the combination of data, creativity and commerce. Amazon used Collaborative Filtering Algorithms to give user recommendations based on customer buying habits and interactions. It all comes down to prediction. The advertisers who predict the best, win.

In a letter to shareholders in 1997, Bezos identified that Amazon are customer focused rather than competitor focused, starting from the customers' needs and working from there.[6]

The emergence of algorithms in marketing

The Amazon team were quick to understand the link between data and purchasing decisions.

In 1997 Greg Linden, Brent Smith and Jeremy York developed and implemented Amazon's revolutionary 'recommendation' algorithm. Amazon proved that how algorithms are written could change the course of a business. This was a foundational moment in data-driven advertising – using data to drive a recommendation. It's not so dissimilar to how the creative brain works: we get inputs, we store those inputs in our brain and when we get a creative challenge, that experience is drawn upon to suggest a creative solution or a recommendation.

Amazon introduced the 'Customers who bought this item also bought' option where the site would use collaborative filtering algorithms to suggest new items from the catalogue.

It's interesting that the primordial version of paid social adverts on your phone came from the primaeval sludge of online book recommendations. Collaborative filtering assumes that people who agreed on something previously will agree in the future and that they are into the same things they liked previously. The system will generate recommendations based on the users' ratings (think thumbs up, starts, views etc). The system finds other users with similar rating behaviours and uses this to make recommendations.

What's interesting is that the machine that gives the recommendation understands the similarity of patterns for ratings at a massive scale but doesn't need to understand what is in the thing itself. So, Netflix will recommend a show for you to watch but it doesn't understand what is in the show. It knows what attributes it has, e.g. drama, actors, western, English etc, but it doesn't feel the movie. It hasn't watched the film like a human has. This starts to mark out the territory lines between humans and machines. Data in advertising isn't experience, it's an attempt to record experience. If an ad gets a click it means that a click happened; it might be a human, it might be a robot (bot), that's all. Nothing else. If it was a human, the click on its own tells us nothing, just that it happened. It's just one single digital moment in time. It's almost meaningless – almost, but not quite. Many clicks over time start to make a picture.

A collaborative filtering algorithm is a way of comparing users' behaviours like purchases, watching, clicking and sharing as a way of finding users who are similar in this regard. This allowed Amazon to successfully recommend products. This technique is basically a standard on all e-commerce sites but this was a radical shift in how websites sold stuff to people. It stemmed from Bezos emphasizing the importance of innovating its platform using the user as the inspiration and not the developers. The core of this product is Recommendation. These things happened in the past and therefore this outcome is likely to happen in the future, so you should do this thing.

The turn of the century

The new foundations of the internet were being laid, and broadband and wireless networks were allowing the internet to seep into the cracks of mainstream life. You could use your phone and the internet at the same time.

Broadband meant that we could download a whole album in the time it takes to download one song with no more downloads getting to 99 per cent and then getting cut off by someone using the phone and you had to start again. Computers were left on overnight to download an ever-increasing number of songs that would be celebrated at breakfast. Where there's more activity, there's more data and there's potential for new ideas.

This upgrade in internet bandwidth meant you could start to stream video. I hope you're old enough to remember 'buffering' – this is where the film you were watching would stop and a spinning wheel would take over, forcing you to decide whether the pain of waiting was worth the entertainment of the film. This happened over and over again, savaging any artistic subtlety that the director had conjured up. Needless to say, habits changed, content flowed and new data was created.

As the 1990s enjoyed being the last decade where the majority of the world wasn't connected to the internet, the advent of broadband meant that advertising content got richer, creative and more interactive. Multimedia became possible, opening up new creative possibilities in ads. Public spaces and businesses rushed to give people online access in their coffee shops to snare more footfall dollars. The upside was that marketers were starting to get new types of data based on the location of their targets. It really got interesting with the launch of 3G networks in the early 2000s and the introduction of smartphones. By the time everyone went giddy for the iPhone in 2007, advertisers had the chance to target users on the move and not just sit at their desk waiting for the internet to download an image like watching a fax spew out a pizza menu. And while this was all going on above ground, below the oceans massive fibre-optic cables were being laid to speed up the internet globally, allowing advertisers to gather and analyse data on a whole new level.

Search engines

The first search engine was called Archie, a geeky play on the word 'archive'. Created by Alan Emtage at McGill University in Montreal, it was a file-searching tool that was a useful solution at the time and laid the path for future search engines.

AltaVista soon followed, which indexed a huge proportion of the web and made it easy to access. It included natural language queries and new fancy multithreaded algorithms. This creative approach to data processing would significantly improve the user experience of the internet.

Yahoo started in 1994 as 'Jerry's Guide to the World Wide Web' by Jerry Yang and David Filo. It was a directory organized as a hierarchy as opposed to just an index. The name Yahoo comes from creatures from the book *Gulliver's Travels* and is an acronym of 'Yet Another Hierarchical Officious Oracle'. This is typical of the goofiness of the early internet pioneers' humour. It wasn't all buttoned down 1s and 0s. Creativity and fun were part of the picture early on.

Google – turning data into dollars

Google was originally called BackRub but the name changed when Sean Anderson suggested 'Googolplex' as a name, a large number that has a 1 and 100 zeros. Larry Page then shortened it to 'Googol'. A quick search to see if the name was available on a registry database ensued. In a happy twist of fate Sean misspelt the name and typed in Google.com. Page liked this accidental creative twist and within hours registered it for himself on 15 September 1997. This moment in its own way was a creative idea that happened and was shaped by data.[7] The team thought of a name (a creative idea) and then tested that name with some data, in this case the registry data on which names had been taken. And then throw in some magic random-ness of a spelling mistake and one of the best-known brand names is born. Without the 'data' of the internet registry Google would have been Googol. Would that have made any difference? Maybe.

The acquisition of DoubleClick

DoubleClick was founded in 1996 and quickly became a powerful provider of services that allowed brands to track and manage ad campaigns on the web. It was very good at helping brands target the right consumers in an efficient way with their ads. In 2006 Google shelled out $3.1 billion for DoubleClick and this was given the green light by the European Union in the midst of moaning from others. This acquisition raised a few eyebrows about privacy and market dominance. Detractors argued that combining search data and DoubleClick's tracking would give Google too much data on users' online actions.

The force of annoyance was so strong that when Google acquired DoubleClick,[8] they had to keep the user data separate between each specific service so data associated with Search would not be combined with data associated with DoubleClick data (although this would reverse in a 2012 policy change).

This was a killer move for Google; much like its move into analytics, it gave Google an ability to play outside of its search engine product. It allowed brands to serve ads from Google that weren't directly associated with search. So, when consumers were on websites that weren't Google, then Google could still serve those ads – this was a lot of power for one company. The cool thing about DoubleClick was its ad exchange that made the buying and selling of ads online efficient. Now that Google had integrated DoubleClick's tech they were able to offer advertisers powerful targeting capabilities. Brands could now understand consumers better, get a sense for their preferences and give more personalized ads. More data, better ideas. They could dramatically improve the effectiveness, measurability and performance of digital media for publishers, advertisers and agencies.

The rise of social media and interactive marketing

Facebook opened for business in 2004 and was only available to Harvard students but let in other students at other Ivy League schools soon after.[9] This was followed by most other universities in Canada and the United States. At this point there were 1 million active users and it was soon to get bigger as Facebook opened its doors to anyone over 13 with a valid email address. In 2006 it was all over for the purely education institution-only Facebook and every man and his dog could get on the platform.

By 2007 Facebook had 20 million users and was a serious consideration for advertisers. Facebook's ad proposition was strong at this point because the nature of the platform meant that they could offer targeting based on rich user data like demographics, interests and social connections. This data enabled highly targeted advertising, a revolutionary approach at the time.

The newsfeed arrived in 2006, which made Facebook a more enjoyable experience for the user but also a new space for advertisers – ads were now part of the flow of content.

In 2004 Facebook launched its first type of ad, called 'Flyers', which were on the homepage and offered local businesses the chance to advertise on specific college campuses. It ramped up significantly after that, with Apple sponsoring a group on Facebook and paying $1 per member per month. This was popular and was reported to have netted Facebook around $100,000 in the first few months. If only all ad sales were that easy. Facebook provided advertisers with real-time data on ad performance, including click-through rates, engagement and conversion metrics.[10] This meant that brands could use this data to do better targeting but also to understand their behaviour better and adapt on the fly. The innovations continued with the roll-out of more sophisticated marketing tools like Custom Audiences and Lookalike audiences, which offered a more precise definition of audiences.

Mid-2000s

Google had a strong search business but in its mission to organize the world's information it thought it prudent to acquire the analytics company Urchin Software. At that point web analytics were slow, expensive and complicated and only available to large corporations. Providing data on how companies' websites were performing was a key missing part of the puzzle for Google and an analytics product would help them close the loop as a tech provider for advertising and marketing. Google could drive clicks for brands and now with analytics they helped brands see what consumers did with those clicks on their website.

Google made analytics available and free to all, allowing businesses and website owners to freely and easily track what was happening on their websites. This was a key moment for online marketing and the market reacted. In November 2005 when it was launched it was so popular that Google had to suspend new sign-ups to cope with the overwhelming demand.

In this period YouTube was born and would end up being one of the giants of data-driven marketing. It was officially activated by Chad Hurley, Steve Chen and Jawed Karim, with video upload functionality in April 2005. The site's original concept was as a video-based dating service, operating under the slogan 'Tune In, Hook Up'. The founders realized that this approach wasn't cutting it. Around this time, they had struggled to find online footage of the infamous 2004 Super Bowl halftime show incident involving Janet Jackson and Justin Timberlake, which revealed a critical gap in online video sharing. Recognizing a larger opportunity, they pivoted away from dating and focused on building a simple, user-friendly platform for uploading and sharing videos. The goal was to create a service that would allow anyone, regardless of tech knowledge, to publish, upload and view streaming videos seamlessly through standard web browsers and modern internet speeds. On 23 April 2005, YouTube's first-ever video, 'Me at the zoo', was uploaded by Karim, featuring himself at the San Diego Zoo.[11]

The personalization era and mobile marketing

In the late 2000s and 2010s we saw the introduction of the idea of social CRM where brands could track brand mentions and customer feedback as part of their data source on customers.

Twenty years ago, the data available to marketers was point-of-sale transactions, responses to direct mail campaigns and coupon redemptions. Big Data changed this and can be described as a data set that is far too large for a person or a group of people to make any sense of manually. It can often be thought of as five Vs:

- Volume – lots of it, typically terabytes or petabytes of data.
- Velocity – the speed with which the data is created and captured is high and requires processing in the moment.
- Variety – the data can come in all shapes and sizes, e.g. photos, videos and text.
- Veracity – is the data trustworthy, is it accurate, is it validated and clean?
- Value – is this data actually useful and can decisions be made off the back of it? If Big Data is used well then the analytics folks can glean consumer insights from this, helping make predictions and improving decision making.

Wielding this type of data started to change how marketers target their audiences. With data on demographics, online behaviour and purchase preferences brands could target people who were more likely to be open to do the things online they wanted them to. Ideally this would make their ads more relevant and increase the efficiency of their marketing efforts.

Marketers could start to use the wealth of new data on what consumers did at different points of the customer journey to create better experiences. This opened up the possibility for decision making to happen quickly.

Leveraging Big Data allowed brands to start to optimize their ad campaigns as they happened. With the ability to collect and analyse large amounts of data on how customers interact with campaigns, brands could start to work out a more precise Return on Investment (ROI) for their campaigns.

In 2013 Big Data was being produced far faster than marketers could deal with, but it did form the foundation of a new type of marketing that would include the use of artificial intelligence, machine learning and automation. At this point marketing started to want to be 'data driven' and the role of data in the creative process began to change.

Data was beginning to move from being something to analyse advertising performance after a campaign to a power that could show brands what was happening in the moment and in a lot more detail. Data was starting to encroach on creative's territory and become a powerful voice in the marketing process.

The two major changes in consumer behaviour in this period were everyone getting excited about smartphones and social media. This created new data on a new scale. Facebook, Google and Amazon started to use this data to create personalized advertising experiences. The dream was that the advertising wouldn't feel like advertising – well, that was the dream at least.

Programmatic advertising

Programmatic advertising is a fancy way of buying and placing ads online using automation. This kicked off with Real Time Bidding around 2009. This allowed ads to be bought online quickly. When a web page loaded in the background advertisers made automated bids for the chance to get their ad on that page. Before this the process was manual and less accurate. This gave the promise of getting the right ad to the right person at the right time.

This was revolutionary as it made the whole process more efficient and gave brands the ability to target audiences based on demographics, online behaviours and their interests. Brands were happy, agencies were happy and so were the publishers who could get more ads sold on their websites. This was a key moment where data started to steal some of creative's ground. Advertisers could now theoretically get their ad in the right place at the right time – did it matter how good the ad was? Once you can target and land the message to a smaller group of people, there's less of a need for a big idea that suits everyone.

Predictive analytics

By the mid-2010s the mindset had shifted from using data to see what happened, to seeing what might happen. Predictive analytics in advertising is the use of algorithms and historical data to predict the type of ad a user may want to see. The appeal to brands was that they could put a different ad in front of different audiences based on the data that they had in a bid to make their products seem more appealing.

In 2012 in a suburb outside Minneapolis an irate man barged into a local Target store seeking to pick a bone with the manager. He was clutching a mailer sent to his high school daughter filled with ads for maternity clothes and baby gear, and he demanded answers. The manager, who wasn't at the forefront of data, creativity and ads, had no clue what was going on. Apologies ensued and the manager even called to apologize at a later date. The father, now with a hint of embarrassment, shared a revelation – she was pregnant.[12]

This story highlights not just the unexpected accuracy of Target's predictive analytics but also the delicate balance companies must navigate with combining creativity and data.

Social listening

Before the digital age transformed how we capture consumer insights, brands depended heavily on traditional methods like focus groups, surveys and in-person feedback to understand what customers thought and felt about their products. These methods came with significant limitations like small sample sizes and inherent biases, leading to less-than-clean data. There was a need for a broader, more accurate gauge of consumer sentiment, a gap that social listening was poised to fill.

The early 2000s saw the rise of social media platforms and brands saw these platforms as a source of data to fuel better creativity.

Social listening offered a unique lens into cultural evolution, presenting a type of data that goes beyond mere observation of digital chatter. It allows for a more nuanced understanding of cultural shifts in ways traditional focus groups and quantitative data alone cannot capture. It's not without its challenges and biases, but it provides a different kind of insight – one that's more empathetic and forward-looking.

At its core, effective advertising is rooted in empathy, understanding, feeling and seeing the world from the consumer's perspective.

The promise of social listening lies in its ability to anticipate the future, allowing brands to detect shifts before they become mainstream. This requires a proactive form of creativity, not just reacting to trends but shaping them. It challenges marketers to view data not as an endpoint but as the starting point for creativity, ideation and innovation.

The wayward untapped power and threat of social media loomed. I had the privilege of working for a business called We Are Social in London during a lot of this period. There was a rush to get creative ideas into this space. There was also a focus on getting data that would help brands understand its impact. Around this time there was the advent of big data and analytics, which transformed customer experience. Once again this was an opportunity and a curse because this gave brands the opportunity to personalize experiences at scale. However, the inherent problem with personalization is that the first time you receive a personalized experience you expect one the next time. And if it isn't there the next time, you notice it not being there.

Mobile marketing and the app explosion

A great example of the harnessing of mobile was the Nike+ running app that used mobile app data to inspire a community, loyalty and new personalized marketing. This wasn't just advertising, but a service blending the lines between utility and persuasion through data-driven insights. Nike were not alone and apps poured in the app stores – it was a creatively rich period where data was central to experience, ideation and messaging.

Starbucks piled in with a mobile app that included mobile ordering, payment, offers and rewards. It used customer data to enhance experience and sales. It used purchase history data and preferences to send tailored messages to users. This used data as a foundation for messages to go out to the audience – 20 per cent of all orders in the United States came via the app in 2019.[13]

The best of the apps blurred the lines between advertising and customer experience. Starbucks has used data creatively to make customer service better, which is its own version of advertising. In other words the service became the message.

The Cambridge Analytica data scandal of 2018 marked a watershed moment in the ongoing struggle to balance data-driven innovation with individual privacy. The company started harvesting vast troves of personal information from Facebook users in their pursuit of building psychographic profiles which could be targeted to influence voter behaviour. The firm vacuumed up intimate details on everything from political views and religious beliefs to relationship status and online shopping habits. The use of this data by political parties laid the groundwork for a sophisticated targeted advertising campaign during the Brexit referendum and the 2016 US election.

When this technique became common knowledge it triggered massive public outrage, as people suddenly grasped the profound implications of surrendering their digital lives to platforms. Where many once saw Facebook as a trusted community to share life's private moments, the reality was much darker and the public's personal data was being weaponized behind the scenes to manipulate electoral outcomes. Understandably, people were not happy with the social media giants claiming to bring us all together while silently influencing the democratic processes for profit.

Regulation has a poor chance of keeping up with technological changes in behaviour in general but this pivotal moment compelled lawmakers and platforms to take user privacy and consent in digital advertising a lot more seriously.[14]

The dawn of chatbots

As of 2025 chatbots have frightening and mostly unchartered power in data-driven marketing. But 10 or so years ago, they were cute. Chatbots allowed for a level of instant customer service at any time of day, providing quick responses to consumers, or at least that's what was promised. This freed up human agents to handle more complex issues and we saw the likes of Sephora creating a chat box on Facebook Messenger to offer personalized beauty advice. Domino's Pizza also released a Dom chat box that will allow you to order a pizza with a single emoji.

Chatbots revealed an interesting relationship between creativity and data. The problem with delivering creativity at scale is that assumptions need to be made about what an audience might want. Most machines can only deliver an aggregated and generic response to a user's input. The downside of this was that chatbots were frustrating. This is an inherent problem between a brand wanting to deliver scale and a consumer desiring an experience that is truly personalized, so brands need to understand that quick and cheap often comes at the expense of good.

The experience economy

Today, we're in the midst of what some call the 'experience economy', where customers value memorable experiences as much as, if not more than, the products or services themselves. Brands that create engaging, seamless and emotionally resonant customer journeys stand out. Apple's product launches have become iconic not just for the innovative products but for the experience surrounding these launches, turning product announcements into major events that fans and media eagerly anticipate.

The explosion of data and automation (2010s–present)

By 2010, marketers had realized that giving all the credit to one ad, whether it was the first impression or the last click, wasn't going to cut it anymore. Multi-Touch Attribution (MTA) stepped in, tracking every single ad a person saw before they made a purchase. This approach became more favourable to brands who could see which social network sparked interest, the role that a search ad played and if a fancy retargeting strategy got the cash in the till.

Around 2013, brands were getting swamped with data from websites, apps, emails and social media and desperately needed a single view of the customer. Enter Customer Data Platforms (CDPs), which gathered all types of data from every touchpoint and attempted to build a profile for each consumer that they had data for. The dream was that instead of hassling you with the same ad repeatedly, brands could now tailor messaging based on your behaviour.

By 2014 consumers were using loads of devices, switching between laptops, smartphones, tablets and even smart TVs. This was great for brands who used Identity Resolution to track consumers across multiple devices. This ensured that if you bought a toilet seat on Saturday you'd see ads for the same toilet seat for weeks afterwards.

In 2015 the practice of sentiment analysis scraped millions of tweets, reviews and social media posts and used machine learning to give brands an indication of what consumers thought of their wares. In theory brands could anticipate PR disasters before they kicked off and adjust messaging on the fly.

The practice of analysing the vapour trails of online conversation and behaviour created enough data to be able to make predictions about the future. Around 2016 brands were using this technology to work out where trends were going and ideally create them.

If inventing the future wasn't enough, in 2017 we started looking inside consumers' brains. The promise of neuromarketing was that brands could use EEG scans, fMRI and eye-tracking software to see how consumers involuntarily responded to ads.

By 2018 Dynamic Creative Optimization (DCO) was becoming popular to test multiple variants of visuals and copy in live ads, depending on who was looking at it. Automated Creative was founded at this time to combine the strategic thinking of an agency with the power of dynamic advertising.

Around 2019 the industry felt privacy laws tightening and the everlasting promise of the death of third-party cookies loomed. Brands needed a way to target consumers without collecting personal data. Data Clean Rooms allowed companies to get insights into their customers without exposing individual user data.

5G and the expansion of AR/VR ads in the 2020s

The arrival of 5G brands started rolling out magical 3D shopping experiences and virtual reality brand activations. IKEA let you place virtual furniture in your home, Nike let you try on shoes with AR and Snapchat turned selfies into branded experiences. The future of advertising wasn't just about seeing ads, it was about being the ad.

2020 – present: the era of privacy, AI and the post-cookie web

2021: AI-powered ad creation and hyper-personalization

By 2021 artificial intelligence wasn't only optimizing ad targeting – Meta, Google and TikTok rolled out AI-driven ad tech that tested different visuals, headlines and calls-to-action to find the most effective combination. This period also saw the start of brands using generative AI to create product descriptions and simple visuals.

2022: The rise of retail media networks – brands become their own ad platforms

In 2022 major retailers like Walmart and Target took a leaf out of Amazon's book and launched Retail Media Networks (RMNs). These platforms let brands buy highly targeted ads using first-party shopper data directly on their e-commerce websites. Retailers went from selling products to selling advertising space.

2023: ChatGPT and the generative AI explosion

In late 2022, ChatGPT brought AI-powered marketing to the mainstream. By 2023, brands were using generative AI for real-time AI-crafted ad creative. Brands like Snapchat, Coca-Cola and Expedia began integrating AI into customer service, ad creation and content marketing,

2024: The rise of zero-party data and privacy-first marketing – consumers take control

With third-party cookies nearly extinct, brands got all excited about zero-party data that consumers proactively share. Loyalty programmes and quizzes became more valuable than ever as brands realized that the future of marketing wasn't about spying on consumers but getting their consent. That took a while.

2025: AI-powered predictive analytics and autonomous marketing

As of 2025, brands are scrambling to be seen to be using generative AI to and to cut the cost of making advertising. Soon enough all brands will be generating their ads and it will be more efficient and cheaper. But then what? Once all the efficiencies have been made the only thing that will matter is creativity, and that's where you come in.

What's next in this book

Looking back at the history of data-driven marketing, one thing is clear: data has always been part of advertising but it's never been the whole story. From Caxton's *Sarum Pie* advert in 1477 to the rise of predictive analytics and AI, marketing has always been about finding ways to persuade people using the best tools available at the time. Whether it was the gut instincts of 19th-century shopkeepers, the focus groups of the 1950s or the digital dashboards of today, data has shaped advertising but it has never replaced creativity.

This chapter has explored how data evolved from anecdotal insights to the overwhelming flood of analytics we see today. What started as scribbled notes on customer behaviour has turned into predictive models and hyper-targeted ads. But despite all the advances, the core challenge remains the same: how do we use data to make better creative work rather than just more efficient ad buys? The danger today isn't that we have too much data, but that we let it take control by measuring what's easy to measure instead of what matters.

This is why the tension between data and creativity runs through the entire book. It's not a question of choosing one over the other but learning how to make them work together. Data has the power to inspire ideas rather than restrict them, to fuel creativity rather than sterilize it. The best marketing has always been a blend of insight and imagination.

Now that we've covered how we got here, the next step is figuring out where we go next. The following chapters will look at the mindsets, teams, research methods and strategies that help brands balance ideas and insight. If history has taught us anything, it's that marketing works best when data and creativity aren't fighting for dominance, but pushing each other to do better work.

KEY TAKEAWAYS

- Data's always been there in marketing, from the very first hand-printed ad to ads made by AI.

- Every new ad tech innovation forces marketers to refine their relationship with data.

- Now you can really bore people at conferences with your marketing history knowledge.

Notes

1 Kwakkel, E (2019) The oldest surviving printed advertisement in English (London, 1477), Medievalbooks, medievalbooks.nl/2019/01/24/the-oldest-surviving-printed-advertisement-in-english-london-1477/ (archived at https://perma.cc/7RH7-YMG7)

2 IBM (nd) The punched card tabulator, www.ibm.com/history/punched-card-tabulator (archived at https://perma.cc/3UBG-QSTW)

3 McCambley, J (2013) The first ever banner ad: why did it work so well? *The Guardian*, 12 December, www.theguardian.com/media-network/media-network-blog/2013/dec/12/first-ever-banner-ad-advertising (archived at https://perma.cc/2SYG-FXRU)

4 Johnson, S (nd) Lou Montulli and the invention of cookie, Hidden Heroes, hiddenheroes.netguru.com/lou-montulli (archived at https://perma.cc/97LN-SNE3)

5 National Science and Media Museum (2020) A Short History of the Internet, www.scienceandmediamuseum.org.uk/objects-and-stories/short-history-internet (archived at https://perma.cc/QC7T-ZFZR)

6 Northboundbrand.com (2025) Delivering on the brand promise of customer-centricity, www.northboundbrand.com/case-studies/amazon (archived at https://perma.cc/ZJ5R-MGJE)

7 Koller, D (2004) Origin of the name 'Google', Stanford.edu, graphics.stanford.edu/~dk/google_name_origin.html (archived at https://perma.cc/NK78-9PQ5)

8   Consumer Watchdog (2016) Google's use of data, consumerwatchdog.org/resources/ftc_google_complaint_12-5-2016docx.pdf (archived at https://perma.cc/7UXP-2AVS)

9   Schneider, A (2004) Facebook expands beyond Harvard, *The Harvard Crimson*, www.thecrimson.com/article/2004/3/1/facebook-expands-beyond-harvard-harvard-students/ (archived at https://perma.cc/4CSG-GLFR)

10   Ibid

11   Alleyne, R (2008) YouTube: Overnight success has sparked a backlash, *The Telegraph*, 31 July, www.telegraph.co.uk/news/uknews/2480280/YouTube-Overnight-success-has-sparked-a-backlash.html

12   Amemiya, C (2025) How Target realized a teen girl was pregnant before her dad knew, Medium, medium.com/illumination/how-target-realized-a-teen-girl-was-pregnant-before-her-dad-knew-42f652d543c9 (archived at https://perma.cc/HHC7-X5QG)

13   Felicia (2018) Mobile App Success Story: Nike+ Run Club, App Sumarai, 9 April, appsamurai.com/blog/mobile-app-success-story-nike-run-club/ (archived at https://perma.cc/LW5P-JSP9)

14   Harbath, K and Fernekes, C (2023) History of the Cambridge Analytica controversy, Bipartisan Policy Center, 16 March, bipartisanpolicy.org/blog/cambridge-analytica-controversy/ (archived at https://perma.cc/J82U-ENL5)

03

Evolving data strategies

The way we use data today would melt the mind of any Mad Men-era marketer. Real-time data, constant tracking, endless dashboards, Gen AI, it never ends. It wasn't always this intense. Here's how we got here, and why it matters now.

In this chapter I'm going to share stories and anecdotes from seasoned veterans who have watched the use of data in advertising evolve over the last 20 years. We'll see that the scale of data is increasing so far beyond marketers' ability to use even a fraction of it. But also that it has been on a slow march from being something we used after a campaign has run to being an important consideration at each stage of marketing.

The dawn of web analytics

Around 1998 Jim Sterne witnessed the dawn of web analytics, which meant that companies could analyse the performance of a website by measuring customer experience and seeing if changing things to the site would improve its usability. This led him to write a white paper with Matt Cutler on web analytics called 'E Metrics'. They interviewed 25 companies, asking how they measured their websites' success, and all of them said that they had too much data and no clue what to do with all of it. That was nearly 30 years ago. The amount of data that has become available since then would be enough for thousands of years' worth of campaigns. This volume of data is unimaginable, but our task as marketers is to make sense of it and make it useful.

Marketing's uncomfortable truth

There's a school of thought that argues that much of marketing persuades people away from the most logical or beneficial choice. We don't always sell the best product, we sell the one we're paid to sell. While this is part of the job, it raises difficult questions about ethics that are too often ignored. The marketing world sometimes seems willing to prioritize optics over impact, selling not only products, but also stories about those products, to itself.

Creativity over integrity

A story that exemplifies the deceptive nature of some people in our industry happened at a famous advertising awards ceremony. A prestigious prize was awarded to a campaign for a brand in South America that cleverly reused some legacy infrastructure to great effect for less fortunate people in that nation. A source told me that they reached out to the CMO of the brand and asked for more detail on the campaign. The CMO informed them that the campaign never happened, never went live. The organization responsible for the submission had asked if they could submit the concept for awards. All the data was made up and ego and ambition took over. If this story is true, the industry's need for accolades will let creativity steamroller data. So much so in fact that the data for this campaign could have been completely made up.

But it's not all bad like this. Founder of Working Media, Sam Gaunt, says:

> The digital world is awash with data which reveals how long people spend with a brand's assets, how they interact with those assets and how they interact with whatever it is advertising. There's so much insight you can get from that. I think that's the great shift in media consumption from offline to digital. Over the last couple of decades that's what's really driven this huge explosion in data.

eBay's PPC reality check

But the data can lead us down the wrong path. A well-documented story tells of when eBay ran an experiment in 2013 where they turned off their paid search ads for brand-related keywords and they found a shockingly low impact on sales. They found that many of the clicks they were paying for through PPC (pay-per-click) were actually coming from people who would have gone to eBay anyway. They were paying millions for users visiting the site anyway, meaning the spend wasn't actually driving any meaningful value.[1]

The findings from this experiment challenged the assumption that PPC always provides a return on investment and highlighted the importance of analysing the true incremental value of paid media. The results helped reshape the way marketers approach their paid search strategies, particularly for branded keywords.

The key takeaway here was that brands, especially large ones, need to analyse whether PPC is truly adding incremental value or just capturing clicks that would happen regardless.

Revealing audience truths

Data sheds light on the dark and can reveal new unexpected truths about the audiences we want to persuade. Global CEO of MS/SIX & Partners, Jess Burley, recalls:

> When programmatic advertising was really starting to emerge, we realized that we were actually able to build audience targeting and survey audiences in a completely different way from the traditional methods of demographic or psychographic profiles. Actually, in a single ID there were north of 1,000, 2,000 data points within any ID within the digital environment. As soon as you get that level of granularity, your ability to test something extensively can be quite challenging because you've got such a deep data source to lean on. That was a turning point. And for our experience at that time, we had to invent a new role. Until then, everybody had talked about psychographics and demographics. From that moment on, we talked about individual IDs and cohorts.

The double-edged sword of data

Data creates a great source of knowledge but also a great processing problem. Data only captures something that has happened, that's it. And the interpretation of the thing that happened. Lots of data is relatively easy to capture. So now advertisers have lakes of data that can be interpreted in different ways. This makes data susceptible to the agenda of the individual who is presenting it. It would be handy if data could be limited to 1s and 0s but data is the record of something happening. So as humans we are collectors of all kinds of unstructured and untrustworthy data from all of our senses.

From numbers to sentiments

Professor of Business, Jagdish Sheth, explained to me how the nature of data has changed drastically over his career: 'Data went from alphanumeric, which I grew up with, to increasingly unstructured data – sentiments. People now express their views in English rather than ticking a box on a numerical scale.' This shift back to qualitative data reminded him of earlier days in market research: 'In the past, when we conducted surveys or focus groups, we asked people to explain or describe their opinions. It was always unstructured data, rich with insights but tricky to measure.' Social media, according to Jagdish, amplified this trend significantly: 'Social media became a platform that unravelled what's truly in the mind of the consumer – not just *what* they buy, but *why* they buy it. That distinction is crucial.' Now, we're not just tracking transactions, we're exploring motivations and post-purchase emotions. 'We've shifted from numerical to non-numerical data, and this gives marketers far deeper insights into consumer satisfaction and buying rationale.' This shift is profound. We've moved beyond raw numbers and back towards understanding real human feelings, where marketing began.

Big data: overpromised or underdelivered?

The opportunity that access to data presented to marketers originally showed great promise but has it really helped? The data 'big bang' has created the opportunity for new kinds of challenger brands to emerge and succeed at a smaller size but has it been as productive for the larger corporations? Marketing consultant Peter Field holds a negative position on a lot of the data that advertisers are being sold:

> If you look at global data around spend, you see that digital spend has now overtaken TV and so forth and this has effectively been a negative trend. We can see from the data that the more money that brands switched out of traditional media and into digital platforms, the lower the effectiveness. It's not a good trend.
>
> What's really been going on in the world of marketing is a schism between small unbranded businesses, people working out of their back room, their bedroom or wherever. Selling products to the world and very sensibly using digital media to be able to do that because it gives them the ability to absolutely control their costs and target and make investments at the speed that they can.
>
> There's a big difference between that and the world of big, branded, multinational business. If you look at the data that I work with, effectiveness data, which does tend to be based in big brand marketing, then you see something very different. TV is quite solid amongst those kinds of advertisers.

Peter's view is that apart from YouTube, which can be a useful storytelling platform, 'Most digital platforms are profoundly less effective at storytelling than traditional media such as TV and print.' His view, based on research, is that there is a gradual drift away from the use of proven effective storytelling mediums. He goes so far as to say, 'Social media is pretty lousy at telling stories, frankly – it depends on the feed and how they serve the ad, but "in-feed" is absolutely rubbish.'

Data empowering creativity

Peter's perspective contrasts with AI-energized Executive Creative Director Becky McOwen-Banks's view that these digital data signals are of great use to a creative. She told me, 'Now data is seen as an input, not the measure of an output, it's no longer a closed box. We can now find data for virtually anything about how that audience consumes media.' Becky relies on data that will give her insight. For instance, she says, 'We shouldn't produce any work that's longer than six seconds because people will be on a commute.' The data in the creative brief becomes part of the media deployment at the end of the creative process. Data informs the creative and the creative in turn informs future creative. This isn't a process for the sake of it but, as Becky points out, 'It helps you think of which ideas would be more sticky for the target audience you're talking about.'

At a high level, telling a CMO that their click-through rate has gone up isn't hugely valuable to the business. However, giving data to a creative team on which visual and written elements of their creative are driving positive media outcomes will help make a huge difference to future creative decisions.

When data misleads creativity

Peter Field has a different view:

> The use of data in the form of quant feedback on advertising to improve it
> and make sure we execute well, that used to be, I think, very unhelpful, but
> is now increasingly helpful. If you look back 20 years ago, when the kind of
> data that testing methodologies gave us on creative ideas was very much about
> information and short-term response, I think it was profoundly unhelpful. In
> fact, it led to less effective advertising.

I asked Peter about what his view was on the fact that at the time of writing the advertising spend was moving away from traditional channels to digital. He responded by saying:

> I work with marketers who are looking at that kind of simple finding and
> saying, 'Oh God, well, we need to mimic that (follow the trend of digital spend

moving from TV), we need to put more than 50 per cent of our budget into digital.' It just doesn't follow and it's a total non sequitur, frankly. But, you know, that's another issue. So yes, we have to understand how we tell stories on digital media, because it's growing. And it's growing often for the wrong reasons.

The lost art of storytelling

Peter is in no way anti-digital, he's just against ads that don't tell stories. His view is that you can't build a brand with static ads and short-form videos. He laments the well-documented performance of Adidas, who, he says:

> went heavily down the performance marketing short-term route because they drank the Kool Aid of the performance marketing world in the short term. But then they did some proper long-term market mix modelling and that taught them that 60 per cent of their sales growth came not from the performance marketing they were doing, but from the brand building that they had been walking away from.

Rethinking the marketing funnel

Marketers today exist in a world where we love to bounce between awareness, consideration and conversion ads, but it's a model that doesn't stand up to much scrutiny. All awareness and consideration ads could directly lead to a sale, all consideration and conversion ads can raise awareness, all awareness and conversion ads can drive consideration. The intended purpose of an ad is, annoyingly, a far cry from what it ends up delivering for the brand. And data that proves which ad drove which action is still far from an exact science.

Quantifying media's impact

While speaking to Sam Gaunt he explained that:

> When I was a media planner, and I worked with a giant fast food retailer, they'd asked me to look into their econometric modelling, which was quite a new-fangled innovation at that time. They wanted to see how we could make use of this statistical way of understanding the correlation between different data points, particularly the impact between media spend and sales. So, I was playing around with this and said, 'Okay, what value can we get from it?' Then I realized that one of the great outputs from econometric modelling is getting

these response curves back. Then you can understand the sales impact from every dollar that you spend and how that diminishes as you spend more and you can map that versus different media channels. That was an 'aha' moment for me because then I realized there is a way of actually understanding the impact of investment. I think that up to that point I had noticed marketing seemed to be full of opinions, and probably still is and it's not a bad thing. When I think back 15 or 20 years, there wasn't data to help verify people's hypotheses or understand the effect of these kinds of decisions. So, there was a point when I realized: there's actually data out there that looks at consumer behaviour. At that point I realized okay, there's opportunities here to really understand the real-world impact on behaviour of marketing decisions.

REAL-WORLD EXAMPLE
Behind Burger King's magic

In the last 20 years the usefulness of data has improved to help brands understand what is happening at a higher level. But how data is used at a creative ideation level has changed as well. Tiffany Rolfe gave me insight into Subservient Chicken, which was a famous campaign for Burger King that her agency worked on. It was a great example of when the use of data isn't obvious in the execution of the idea. Rolfe told me, 'When there's great data, it can turn into magic, right? Technology and data together can actually make people believe there's real magic, if you bring that in.'

The Subservient Chicken campaign gives an interesting perspective on data because the idea was simple, and based on the product promise of 'It's a chicken, your way'. The idea was a website where you can type in commands to dress someone up as a chicken and you can then tell it what to do whatever you want. This was 2004, a good 20 years before generative AI. 'So now we're in a place where data is actually magic. This was pre-AI.' It worked; somehow the chicken would do anything you asked it to do, like dance, play dead, sleep, roll over, walk like an Egyptian, flap wings, do push-ups, take a bow, do a backflip (though it didn't actually perform a full flip, it mimicked trying), just about anything, and no one could work out how they did it. But if the command didn't match a pre-recorded video, the chicken would respond in a humorous way, like tilting its head in confusion or ignoring the command entirely.

Rolfe reveals the parlour trick's secrets:

They basically surveyed everyone in the agency and asked, 'What would you have someone do if they were in a chicken suit?' Around 1,000 agency people wrote back and the team made a list of all the things that they would have a chicken do.

What was wild is that 99 per cent of people said the same 10 things, which is like, lay an egg, you know, roll over, flap your wings.

They ended up with a data set that revealed the insight that just a few actions came up '99 per cent of the time'. This data made Rolfe realize that we are all not as unique as we think.

Rolfe told me that:

When they programmed it people thought it was a live experience, this was pre-live, this is pre-anything, but it was based on data that people are going to say a certain thing. They're going to do a certain thing and you can create an experience that anticipates and actually gives them magic.

Rolfe's view was that people feel they are unique and their demands of the chicken would be unique but when it comes to ordering around an actor in a chicken suit, we've got similar desires. So, the creative team were able to create an experience that felt very unique based on understanding people and what they'll do.

For Rolfe this is an example of an interesting insight into data:

It was insight into human behaviour, a potential need or response, and they were able to create and design an experience that answered that for people. It was really just having a good data set, not guessing and anticipating. It was really digging into what people would do in that scenario. So that, to me, it is an example of using data in an interesting way to create a unique experience and get some magic.

The campaign was picked up by mainstream media and became a legend in its own time. It even has its own Wikipedia page. Rolfe now reflects on how her role has changed over the years since advertising started: 'Advertisers are no longer in a broad media type of environment.' Now brands need to address 'niche communities and connect with people that aren't like yourselves, that are maybe from diverse backgrounds, different parts of the world'. This means that the 'limited data set' of our own experiences of life is woefully unfit for the task. Data is the only way we can expect to get anywhere near the perspective that we need to have any empathy for the audiences we want to persuade.

Programmatic advertising's data revolution

Jess Burley took me forward from the days when bossing poultry around was a successful idea to the start of programmatic advertising:

Around 2010, when programmatic advertising was really starting to emerge – the realization that we were able to build audience targeting and therefore survey those audiences in a completely different way from the traditional methods of demographic or psychographic profiles.

This was a turning point for Burley and new roles needed to be invented.

Data paralysis in advertising

Data has answers but immediately the question is raised of what data to use. Digital business consultant Tom Goodwin's view is:

> We now have so much data and there is an overwhelming sense in the industry that data has the answers. We've gone from making a great ad and putting it on TV then six months later when sales are doing alright, we take a bow. That's obviously not a sophisticated approach, but that's how advertising worked for decades. Then it went to the process of pre-testing on the copy to make sure it's good, then sorting focus groups when the ad goes out to make sure that you're responding to people. That seems sensible, but we've almost gone completely the other way, where you can't do anything unless you have data to support it.

The most important change that has happened is that data is no longer something you look at after the run of a campaign. Becky McOwen-Banks told me that earlier in her career, data had always been focused on analysing the results of a campaign. Over the years she's seen that data is stepping backwards from the end of the process and is now an integral part of all stages.

KEY TAKEAWAYS

- Data went from historically sitting quietly in the background of marketing to calling the shots.
- Be careful trusting data without context – remember eBay's expensive mistake.
- Stay curious and adapt or get left behind.

Note

1 Search Laboratory (2013) eBay Report Sells PPC Short, www.searchlaboratory. com/2013/03/ebay-report-sells-ppc-short/ (archived at https://perma.cc/8UZD-37F6)

04

The power couple: data and creativity

All right, cards on the table – this chapter is home to the core idea of this entire book. Why on earth should marketers bother mixing creativity with data? Simple answer: because when it's done right, it'll help the brand you represent sell more.

The problem with best practice

Automated Creative ran a campaign for an infant formula brand a few years ago and the results were so surprising I still tell that story today. Our goal was to sell formula directly to the consumer on the company's own website, cutting out the large online retailers. We came up with a data strategy that centred around a test and learn campaign to seek out which visuals and written themes actually drove sales. The ads were targeted on Facebook to mums, as you might expect. However, the client was shocked to find out that the best-performing visual theme that drove sales – was dads. This wasn't a theory or a hunch but a proven fact, that mums in this market would buy more product when shown an image of a dad.

The result of this campaign may seem odd but in fact it's explainable by one of the industry's worst habits – best practice. This is the habit of brands seeing what other successful brands are doing and copying them. Which means all brands are doing the same thing, and if they are all doing the same thing then no one is marketing, which is the practice of standing out from the market. The 'best practice' for an infant formula would be to use an image of a mum and a baby because the most common and successful ads do this. But the data we collected proved the opposite was true – dads made the brand get noticed, got their ads clicked on and purchases made.

We've seen data and creativity regularly reveal this kind of truth over the last eight years at Automated Creative. We've seen over and over that data can reveal new truths about audiences and can inspire new creative ideas that can build brands and sell. This is why combining data and creativity is a good idea; data can take us far beyond the limited data sets of our own experience and give us insight into what might make our brands favourable to the audiences we seek to persuade.

Customer centricity or Cannes centricity

Nothing makes my eyes roll back in my head faster than a marketer at a conference saying they should put the customer at the centre of their marketing or trying to spice it up by calling it 'customer centricity'. I'm always tempted to say, 'What's the alternative – blind guesswork?' Or maybe the alternative is to try to win awards so you can get a new job and earn more money, in which case something like 'Cannes centricity' could be accurate. I can see the attraction of walking down the Croisette in Cannes sweating profusely while you head up to the Palais to collect your gong, but that's not our job. Our job is to sell.

Creating marketing that is designed around the needs of the person seeing our marketing – that is the game we're in. So, let's stop declaring this as a strategy, it's not. It's the goal. Chaired Professor of Corporate Innovation at INSEAD, Amitava Chattopadhyay, puts this simply: 'True customer centricity helps you actually make money. That means putting the customer first and solving their problem, which then leads you to make money. Saying "How can I make money off these customers?" does not.' Combining data and creativity in a clever way will allow your marketing to help solve a problem for your audiences in a way that is good for them and the brand you represent.

Creativity and data are often seen as opposing forces. Everyone loves creativity for its ability to surprise, engage and make rainbows come out of our ears, while data is deeply respected for its alleged precision, reliability and confidence. You may think that these two forces are incompatible. But in my experience, data doesn't constrain creativity – it catalyses it. As Creative Director Tash Beecher aptly describes, 'Some of the best advertising in the world wouldn't exist without creatives embracing data. The most emotional or impactful campaigns are those that seamlessly blend data and creativity.'

From bourbon to benchmarks

For years, marketers swilled bourbon at their desks and relied heavily on intuition and gut instinct. While this approach created the campaigns that in some way led us to our careers in marketing, they may have lacked the flexibility needed to make sure those ideas worked on all platforms for all people at all times. Data has introduced a scorecard for creative work, enabling marketers to craft campaigns that not only do the emotional job but also deliver measurable results. Sam Gaunt captures this synergy well, noting, 'Data can empower creativity. At its best, data is real-world behaviour from consumers. It can reveal their motivations, behaviours, and perceptions around the brand.' With data, creativity has the potential to be grounded in some form of reality, allowing marketers to create work that is linked to something real rather than assumed consumer behaviours.

Data as a catalyst, not a constraint

Data lets us peer over the garden fence and through the kitchen windows of consumers into their minds, or at least that's what it promises. It helps uncover insights that would otherwise remain hidden, guiding marketers toward creative strategies that have real impact. Peter Field explains the role of data succinctly: 'Data can help generate insights and sharpen strategy, allowing us to understand whether we're executing well and, if necessary, adjust our approach.' This approach to data is not about dampening creativity or following a prescribed route – there are many paths up the marketing mountain – but data can be our guide.

Chief Marketing and Digital Officer Lex Bradshaw-Zanger gave an example of this when talking about the McDonald's 'Raise Your Arches' campaign. It perfectly demonstrated the unexpected insights data could reveal. Research showed that the most emotional part of a McDonald's experience wasn't the first bite but rather the moment someone suggested going to McDonald's. This finding led to a campaign that didn't showcase the product itself but rather focused on the simple, relatable gesture of waggling eyebrows – a cheeky invitation to go to the restaurant. The campaign led to a measurable increase in sales. This level of insight could only come from a blend of creativity and data-driven understanding, enabling McDonald's to connect with consumers in their language.

Challenging the taboo – data to enhance creativity

If you ignore the data on how much better creativity can be when using it then it's easy to see how data still faces scepticism from creatives. CEO of Seenapse, Rafa Jiménez, shares how some creative professionals he knows view data with suspicion, 'If technology is assisting them, it's almost like cheating. Creatives have a sense of purity, where they believe that technology dilutes their uniqueness.' This 'purist' mindset overlooks the fact that data is already woven into many creative tools. From Photoshop to video editing software, creatives have long embraced technology to enhance their work. Yet, when it comes to data, a mental barrier persists.

However, not all creatives view data this way. Becky McOwen-Banks argues for the opportunities data gives brands for storytelling: 'The story must meet the scenario, and data is our device to do that.' Rather than being restrictive, data becomes a tool for relevance, enabling brands to connect with audiences at the right moments and through the right channels. In today's fragmented media landscape, where consumers are spread across various platforms, data allows marketers to tailor their messaging based on real-time insights rather than guesses. Observation beats assumption.

Data as an accountability partner

Data can inspire the creative process, but it can continue to play a vital role in evaluating and refining the creative nature of the campaign. As CEO of CreativeX, Anastasia Leng, observes, 'Data can be used to answer a lot of other questions that shape how a brand shows up in the market. It helps us ensure that we're saying what we think we're saying or appearing the way we intend to.' In an era where there is an ever-increasing volume of content needed, maintaining creative effectiveness is challenging. Especially when campaigns are required to span multiple platforms, audiences and markets, raise awareness and make consumers consider buying a product then actually follow through.

Leng tells the story of a high street bank in the UK that prided itself on being the most diverse lender. Yet, an analysis of its creative assets over two years revealed a stark inconsistency: not a single ad featured a person of colour. This wasn't due to a lack of commitment but rather a fragmented content creation process. Data provided a reality check, highlighting the need for structural changes to ensure that the brand's values were accurately represented across all marketing materials. Without data, this misalignment might have gone unnoticed, eroding trust in the brand's diversity claims over time.

Similarly, Leng explained Heineken's approach to leveraging data, demonstrating the potential for data to inform and refine creative frameworks. By analysing tens of thousands of ads, Heineken identified four core attributes that positively correlated with brand lift. This insight allowed the brand to develop a structured yet flexible framework, where creative teams could experiment within a set of parameters known to drive results. Data didn't limit creativity; it gave teams the confidence to innovate within a proven framework, increasing the likelihood of success without stifling the creative process.

Starting with a hypothesis

While data can provide invaluable insights, it requires a structured approach to be genuinely effective. Sam Gaunt emphasizes the importance of having a clear hypothesis: 'You need hypotheses. If you're trying something new and you don't have any existing data to support or disprove that hypothesis, then you should be running an experiment.' This scientific approach to marketing not only grounds creative work in reality but also fosters a culture of continuous learning and improvement.

Testing hypotheses enables brands to refine their messaging and creative direction consistently, allowing them to respond to shifts in consumer behaviour and preferences. This process transforms marketing from a one-time campaign into an ongoing dialogue with the audience, where data continuously informs and enriches the creative approach.

Data-driven marketing as a competitive edge

In a highly competitive landscape, brands cannot afford to ignore any tool that offers an edge. As Jon Williams asserts, brands should 'use everything at their disposal to gain a competitive edge in an environment that is volatile'. Data, he argues, is one of those critical tools. It doesn't replace creativity but rather serves as a reinforcement, providing insights that make campaigns both beautiful and effective. 'It's going to be beautiful. Yeah, it's going to be differentiated. But it's got to work and that's all we're using it for.' By embracing data, brands can ensure that their creative efforts lead to tangible outcomes, whether it's higher engagement, increased sales or a stronger brand perception.

Consider the success metrics Williams cites: 'We get 75 per cent-plus purchase intent on everything that we do. That's why we're seeing a 32 per cent sales uplift on a bag of flour in a supermarket aisle in the West Coast of the US.' Data-driven insights empower marketers to set benchmarks, measure impact and iterate based on real results, creating a feedback loop that continuously enhances campaign effectiveness.

The power of data-driven creativity is perhaps best illustrated through real-world campaigns that used data as a foundation for emotional storytelling. Tash Beecher references a campaign in the healthcare sector, which tackled the issue of women's pain being taken less seriously than men's. Instead of creating a traditional white paper, the campaign launched an emotional platform that connected deeply with both healthcare professionals and patients, shifting perceptions and igniting change. This approach exemplifies the potential of data to move beyond mere numbers, inspiring campaigns that not only inform but also create meaningful social impact.

A new paradigm for marketing

As marketing becomes more complex, the teaming up of data and creativity is no longer a niche pursuit, it's a necessity. Data offers a roadmap, guiding marketers toward insights that resonate with consumers and enhancing the creative process rather than diminishing it. As one of the leading voices in the creative business world, Jon Williams, aptly puts it, 'We need to embrace data. We need to embrace what comes from machines and be confident in the ideas that we're having.'

Data removes doubt, providing a foundation for creativity to flourish in ways that are both emotionally resonant and effective. By grounding creativity in data-driven insights, brands can create campaigns that not only capture attention but also drive lasting impact. In the following chapters, we'll explore how industry leaders have successfully implemented data-driven marketing strategies, demonstrating the immense potential of combining data with creativity to stunning effect.

KEY TAKEAWAYS

- Great marketing combines data rigour with creative risk.
- Data is your best mate, not your boss – use it to inspire and not instruct.
- The best ads happen when data reveals something totally surprising.

05

Mindset mastery: data meets creativity – part 1

Getting your head in the game

Psychology has been acknowledged as its own separate scientific discipline for around a century. The fun and games are widely considered to have kicked off around 1879, when Wilhelm Wundt, a German psychologist, established the first laboratory specifically for psychological research at the University of Leipzig.[1] So, we've not been thinking about the brain scientifically for *that long* and what we'd consider modern advertising isn't *too* dissimilar in age. In comparison to other ancient arts and sciences, formal psychology and advertising are the new kids on the block, so it's not surprising that we haven't got it all figured out yet.

Our best chance of figuring it out when thinking about advertising is making better ads for brands with the use of data. If we combine data with creativity in advertising, we combine the full force of human creativity with the miraculous power of new marketing machines that have been placed into our hands over the last few decades. Like it or not, we're all lab rats in a giant experiment where the rules keep changing and the end is uncertain. But the curious and the bold will be rewarded as we all teeter forward cautiously like a blindfolded child at a party trying to pin the tail on the donkey.

In this chapter I'm going to share advice on the kind of mindset you should have when it comes to data, ads and creativity. There is no rule book, no printable PDF – I'm sorry but it's messy. So tuck in.

'Our job is to waste'

Chief Transformation Officer at Mourant, Tom Grogan's vision is to help his clients be commercially viable, creative and legally compliant – it's not a mix you hear often. Tom brings to the table a narrative that challenges conventional wisdom and pushes the boundaries of what's normal and accepted in marketing. His journey, from software engineer to lawyer at prestigious firms and finally as the CEO of a tech consultancy, underpins a story not just of career evolution but of the evolving landscape of advertising itself.

Grogan was at the Cannes Lions International Festival of Creativity and was discussing advertising at a round table discussion with several big names in the industry. He told me about a moment which shaped his truth-focused approach to consultancy: 'Someone around the table said, *"Tom, you don't understand. We're advertising. Our job is to waste."* And it absolutely blew my mind.'

Tom's reaction to this epiphany was not just of shock but of resolve, leading him to become outcome focused with his clients. He underscores the necessity of this shift, stating, 'There is a desperate need for data measurability in advertising and marketing. And there are too few people doing it.'

It's a tense time for most marketers to read this because 'where there is mystery there's margin' and a lot of the industry is quite happy to sell black boxes and hide in three-letter acronyms with vagueness *just* because a practice is commonplace, That doesn't make it right. Doing something that works is hard enough and doing something that is ethical is even more complicated, but that's what we must do. If there are senior executives silently accepting in Cannes that 'our job is to waste' then we have a problem!

Advertising: problem vs puzzle

Alex Jenkins changed the way I think about data, creativity and marketing when he said that 'advertising is a problem, not a puzzle'. In his eyes there's only one way to solve a puzzle but a problem can be solved many ways. He reminded me that in the 1990s brands sold us beer by having jocks screaming 'whaaattssaaaaapppp' down the phone. In the next ad we would see black and white horses running in the waves with surfers. There are thousands of ads that attempt to solve the problem of selling beer, whereas puzzles have far fewer solutions.

Despite this, the combination of data and creativity is often seen as a puzzle. There's an idea that if you get the right system of technology in place you can solve the puzzle of making effective ads. This view ignores the almost intangible human factor, the almost unfathomable practice of understanding humans and the near-impossible task of trying to get anyone to do anything. We barely know ourselves at times, so the idea that a marketer can even understand a fraction of what is going on in a consumer's head at all is a stretch, let alone get them to do something – it's an uphill battle.

Some consumers have the idea that advertising is a powerful and manipulative force that transcends consumer liberties, and measures like GDPR have been put in place to protect the vulnerable masses from our industry's omnipotence. In reality our gains can be miniscule. I've seen great 'hurrahs' be exclaimed when a lowly banner ad sees an increased improvement in performance by hundredths of a per cent. I often worry that if we rounded up the numbers on some people's performance data slightly then nothing would work at all. Yet it does.

Or, as Vice Chairman of Ogilvy UK, Rory Sutherland, puts it, 'You can't buy what you don't know exists. So remember, some advertising works.'

Is your problem a marketing problem?

Before we get into the practical application of data and creativity in advertising it's worth asking if we are ready to start using it at all. Simon Kemp is the CEO and founder of Kepios and has a provocative view. He says marketers need to ask what is actually stopping the business from achieving its goal. 'Maybe my price is too high. Maybe I'm (the product) not available in the right distribution points. Maybe somebody else is doing a switch at the shelf. And if it's a switch at the shelf, then advertising isn't going to fix that.'

Kemp sees that marketing is a little 'broken' and that we have a 'hammer and the nail' problem where marketers think serving more ads is the solution when 'a lot of the time marketing doesn't need more ads'. Kemp's view is that sometimes brands need better execution at a specific point. His take is that advertising, data and creative ideas are not going to solve a business problem that is unrelated to marketing. Marketing is a tool to solve a business problem but it might not actually be the right tool. And if you're running some marketing activity that isn't going to solve a broader issue then your work, by default, can't be effective.

The key here is to use data in the right way. If you know the questions to ask, you can get answers that will inspire the right action. We need to be clear if the business problem is something that marketing can solve. We're here to grow the businesses we represent, not do marketing. The end is growth and marketing is the means. We need to use our marketing skills to expose a solution to the business problem, not blindly do more advertising simply because that's our job.

Some marketers seem to have the mindset to just throw money at advertising rather than building strong foundations in their marketing strategy. For a marketing strategy to work you have to invest, you have to be interesting, you have to care – there has to be give and take. Often marketing doesn't function like that and it should all be about taking, but Kemp tells us that successful businesses will have ties that are built on a foundation of give and take.

He gives the example of his own business, Kepios. The first reports that he published had around 2,000 views and now they have thousands and thousands more. He's never spent any money because the internet has distributed that content for him. However, if he had wanted to get 20 million views in the first year, he could have just paid for it. Kemp understands why people advertise, but in his view, 'Advertising is a tax on the impatient and the boring, you only need to pay to interrupt people if they aren't already seeking you out.' In our current marketing landscape brands often lack the patience to grow in this way.

Know why you are doing what you are doing

A marketing agency's goal should be to drive brand value, not just create art and then find data to support its creation. Grogan contrasts the misuse of untethered creativity in advertising with its rightful place in the arts, presenting a nuanced understanding of both worlds: 'I am a huge proponent of the arts, but to tie art to outcome fundamentally misses the purpose.' He explains that a line must be drawn between art and advertising for art's sake and the commercial objectives of advertising. His practical application of this principle aims to solve the issue that advertising makes very complicated things out of things that should be simple.

Grogan emphasizes simplicity and directness in communication with clients as the key to cutting through industry jargon and complexity. Grogan asks a simple question to help brands get into the right mindset: 'Are brands marketing for a "headline" story, "topline" revenue or for "bottomline" cost cutting? If you're not doing it for one of these reasons, don't do it full stop.'

He asks us to imagine launching an ad campaign for an umbrella during a particularly rainy period of the year. His view is that we can't claim it was our campaign that drove demand, but the rain: 'The world will conspire for and against marketers and we need to be honest about that. We need to have the data to prove which way the wind blows.' Despite this, he believes that 'most clients' problems are not a data problem'. In reflecting on his approach to client relationships and project outcomes, Grogan encapsulates his philosophy: 'If we've done really well, I will be standing there, taking the "well done" from the client. If we've done really badly, I'll be standing there, open and honest, and owning the downside as well.'

Grogan pushes us to reimagine the future of advertising, a future where data, creativity and integrity coalesce to create marketing strategies that are not only effective but also ethical and sustainable. His vision for a more accountable and outcome-driven industry offers a blueprint for marketers and advertisers alike, challenging them to rise above the status quo and strive for a higher standard of excellence in their craft. Looking to the future where creativity will likely be always needed and data isn't going to go away. Honesty, integrity and an unwillingness to be bullied by the mainstream are what make Grogan special. Marketers would do well to make sure their creative ambitions are based on truth, not trend, and that they have real data to back themselves.

Going after your most effective audience

Simon Kemp reminded me of a familiar situation of when marketers come into agencies and say, 'We want to do this campaign, to this audience, on this platform'. He feels like that's the equivalent of going to the doctor and only telling them that they need to prescribe you paracetamol – but any good doctor is going to say, 'Why do you need paracetamol?' If you say to a marketer, 'Your brief is wrong,' often hell can break loose. And if you start questioning a client's brief, a tantrum will soon follow.

Marketers need to be using the right data to identify if they are actually going after the most effective audience in the first place. And that brands don't even need that great a creative idea – you just need to do a half-good job they'll appreciate. And consequently brands could sell way more product.

To conclude this section, we need to remind ourselves that marketing is a means and not an end. The purpose of marketing is not to do marketing for the sake of it just because that's what we've been told to do. It's a tool to solve a business problem, so until we've identified what the business problem really is, as Kemp says, 'It's a bit pointless.' We really need to use the data to make sure that we're asking the right questions to solve the right problems.

Taking control of your data

Marketing remains a complex challenge and the first step is to ask the right questions about the business issues rather than jumping to marketing solutions. The more compelling our products and their positioning, the less heavy lifting our advertising will have to do. But once we engage in the world of ads, we need to treat data as a guide, not a rigid grid that dictates our every move. Data should be our servant, *not* our master.

So, let's assume we know what the hypothetical business problem is that our marketing is in part trying to solve. We're going to need some data, but how do you use data today? Does it empower and inspire you to make better ads? Or does it slap your wrist when your ideas don't fit into pre-defined parameters?

In his book *Voltaire's Bastards*, John Ralston Saul proposed that there are about six valuable human qualities that should be deployed in problem solving: *creativity, common sense, ethics, memory, intuition* and *rationality.*

It's Sutherland's view that we *should* all be using these tools 'fairly abundantly' when problem solving, but in reality we don't: 'What we've done is we've said, "no, no, this is all too complicated and too ambiguous. We'll just make rationality the standard criterion for the application of intelligence" and it's dangerous.'

The 'danger' that Sutherland is outlining is that if we only focus on being *rational* and entirely data focused our marketing may devalue *creativity, common sense, ethics, memory* and *intuition*. If these elements are removed from ads then it's easy to imagine them failing to arouse the desired emotions in our audience.

Data is the record of something happening, not an explanation of what happened.

One of the core messages of this book is that data should support not restrict you. Director of Growth Marketing at Sampl, Adam Wright, describes data perfectly: 'Always work on the principle that data acts as a compass rather than a map. Data needs to guide creativity, but it doesn't dictate creativity.'

You need to make a choice. Are you going to use data to control each of your creative decisions or use it to better understand your audience? My belief is that the best use of data is as a source of inspiration for creative ideas that will stir up the kind of emotions that will make your audience think more favourably about your brand.

Don't get distracted by shiny new objects

With each year, the number of social media platforms increases, giving marketing teams the chance to plant their feet at the inception of a potentially viral network. Marketers are of the belief that that somehow if they identify the next TikTok they'll become the next Duolingo, with them standing on a stage telling everyone how great they are. In opposition to this, Simon Kemp pointed out that, interestingly, four out of five people don't feel represented in advertising and the Baby Boomer generation are responsible for 50 per cent of consumer spending in the United States, even though marketers commonly spend 10 per cent of marketing budgets on them. There are two opportunities here: one is to get on stage and the other is to shift products. Which would you take?

Kemp sees a proclivity in advertising to get distracted by the new 'singing and dancing robot', not because a marketing innovation will solve a brand's marketing problem, but because it's new. At the time of writing everyone is getting excited about the latest Gen AI tool but in reality if you want to increase your revenues by 10 per cent there are 'easy, boring ways of doing that based on the data' according to Kemp.

It frustrates Kemp that marketers want to change what they do too often. His opinion is that if you look at the data about how long ads last in terms of how often you need to refresh them, based on the attention that people pay to them, there's a massive disconnect. Kemp's view is that if you kept running your creative until it really wore out you would save 90 per cent of your marketing budget. You just keep the assets that you've got and make them last five times longer.

CREATIVES AND THE FEAR OF DATA

Data can be scary of course. I have half a mind this year to dress up as a spreadsheet and go trick-or-treating with my daughter for Halloween to see what the reaction might be. At the mention of the word 'data' there are creatives the world over shooting around the room like a deflating party balloon that was accidentally let go, blubbering away until they end up in the corner, shrivelled and covered in spittle.

This certainly isn't true of the new breed of creative. Jon Williams, who is a seasoned and celebrated agency creative, observes that 'I've seen agencies forever, scared of consumers… terrified of Millwood Brown, terrified of Nielsen data, terrified of all this stuff… agencies are scared of being measured, agencies are scared of other people's opinions.'

And this is mirrored by Aaron Howe, who says, 'I still really struggle with the disparaging nature of "if you can track it" – it's less valued.'

However, it is fair to say that creatives are right to reject data when it's not useful. Anastasia Leng's view is:

> You have creative directors having at times a negative view of creative data
> because it gives them insights like 'you should make everything red when your

brand colour's blue'. The data-driven folks feel like the creative folks are not amenable to any kind of data and that's not the case. I actually think a lot of great creative people are hungry for more data, but they want data in the places that they believe are most able to change and adaptable to change that don't compromise either the legacy or the differentiation they're trying to impose through the brand standards that they've set up.

For the data hustlers reading this book, we need to make sure that the data we provide to our creative friends can help them do something. Data that provokes no insight or action isn't data, it's distraction. Heaping a tonne of data into the precious attention time of a creative is not a good use of time. Ask the question – is this data going to be inspiring or is it a distraction?

Jagdish Sheth puts it simply: 'Creativity actually comes from data. Data is just observation of the world.' So make your observations count by making them useful to the person you are sharing them with. Make your audience compelled to greatness when they see your data. In short, beware 'interesting' data and instead search instead for 'insightful' data and don't scare off your creatives.

Bad uses of data

Marketers need to avoid risk aversion

Tiffany Rolfe has a lot to say on this subject:

> I think sometimes we're using data as a way to avoid risk, rather than actually uncover unique insights that help us connect with people more. And that's I think the good and the bad side of data… it's become almost like a safety net rather than a real way to uncover unique insights.
>
> We've gotten to a point where data is removing decision making. It's removing the art and the magic of what creativity needs… to really get people to react, respond in a way… Data is being used more for hindsight and to risk-proof versus uncover new. I'm all about new, and to me, data has the potential to create new, to find new, to uncover new. So the best, most amazing way to connect with people is to surprise them and to deliver something that they didn't expect, you know, to show up in a way that has them feel like they're discovering something themselves. Unfortunately, data has become risk-averse – how do we make sure we only do what's been done before?'

Tiffany sees that data is being used for looking back in hindsight instead of to illuminate the future and create innovative ideas. For Rolfe, 'That's the biggest misstep with data. It has the potential to unlock and be about innovation, unlock new amazing experiences for people… and instead of using it to help us win, we're using it to help us not lose. And you don't win by not by trying not to lose.' Rolfe's view is that 'You win by taking risks to do new things, to try things that haven't been done before. I want data help to help inform those things, versus just helping us to not lose.'

Rolfe is guarded against using data to deliver mediocrity where everybody's doing the same thing. This is easily done when 'everyone has the same set of data and they're using it the same way'. The alternative is not to think 'let's just keep doing what everyone else is doing' and instead leverage data in a way that unlocks new ideas, new experiences. This is what Rolfe believes 'really helps bring creativity forward, versus, I think right now it's potentially being used to hold it back'.

Rolfe argues that this situation is being exacerbated by AI, which has the 'potential to unlock new kinds of experiences that we haven't seen before, but also has the potential to just create more of the same, easier and faster, where everybody starts to look the same. And what we're going to get is brands that don't stand out… more and more brands doing pretty okay, rather than the ones that can really stand out and deliver something new, different, and be on their own.' Rolfe's advice to brands is that they should be 'leveraging data to take risks versus leveraging it to stay safe and keep doing more of the same'. Her advice is 'to get it out of the safety zone and the hindsight zone' and into a winning one.

Alex Jenkins sees creativity as a totally different beast to the other 'functional' elements of a marketer's job. Jenkins thinks this fear causes marketers to use data simply to 'see what is going on in the category'. For example, they may be going into advertising archives to copy the tropes of their category, rather than coming up with new ideas. In this way, they end up 'aiming for not-sh*t – rather than actually good'.

Sutherland's take on this is that 'there is a very good argument, which was made by the creative director Andrew Cracknell, that when you come in as a senior creative director, your job isn't to make the good work brilliant, it's to make the worst work better'. This doesn't mean creativity has to be daredevil. But it does mean we should use data to help you create something surprising, not to play it safe.

Misinterpretation of data

Becky McOwen-Banks warns that data is open to deliberate misinterpretation. The practice of reading data in a way that suits our own goals is very common in the advertising industry. This isn't good form, it's deceptive. She asks us instead to be 'honest and dispassionate'.

The mistake is to give too much power to data and to use it in the wrong way. I've seen 'war rooms' filled with ugly monitors that track the speed, sentiment and scale of social media activity to help brands feel they are observing what's happening out there. In these rooms data is there to make the client feel they are doing something meaningful with data. There's an idea that if there is a large volume of data then that increases our chances of finding a useful needle of something in a giant data haystack. Turning off all of those monitors isn't the equivalent of closing our eyes to our consumers. It's the equivalent of forcing us to really look, to really listen to what real people are saying.

Fitting data to pre-existing motivations

But the worst crime I saw over and over again at agencies was to see strategy teams take the creatives' idea and retrospectively fit the insight and consequently the data to the idea.

Don't get me wrong – suppliers are compelled to win pitches by any means necessary and pitches are winner-take-all bloodsports where junior teams get wheeled out to puff up the egos of clients in a battle to the death of who has the best free ideas. So I'm not against winning by any means, but finding data to justify a random idea you had isn't the best way to use data, in a pitch or otherwise.

Data should be used to break new ground, not paper over the cracks. Or, as Sam Gaunt puts it, 'The worst thing to do is to use data to be self-serving against... an already defined kind of outcome.' Using data to justify a view or using it to retrospectively justify a choice can be quite creative but it doesn't open any doors. If you are using data to justify your gut feel then you're closing yourself off to what is really happening in the lives of consumers. This is the opposite of what we should be doing. We need to first be open and empathetic to the lives of our target, that's where the good stuff is. When we really listen, we really care. As Rupert Slade puts it, 'The consumer is who you live and die by... the data tells you stuff about people. Too often data is used to justify expenditures post-rationally.'

Don't use data in isolation

We shouldn't get the data to be the slave to our ideas once we've already had them – this just means we are missing out on the good stuff. But the opposite is also true – we can't be ruled by the data either. When I interviewed Tina Eskridge she said that data should be used to give insight and perspective and not be a 'pressure cooker' making everyone's lives miserable. She continues: 'The reality of using only data is that you have blind spots in data; I could realistically create my own hypothesis out of some data. And it could be lacking in contextual relevance and… so many other things that go into interpreting that data.'

A good example of this comes from Barbara Galiza, who has a story of working on a 'personal financial management app' which helped users combine their bank accounts within the app. She ran ads that talked about the 'combining accounts feature' and ads that talked about 'better fees' to the same audience. The second set performed much better and drove a better click-through rate and cost per click. However, the customers who arrived from the second set didn't stick around and connect their bank accounts and the cost per activated account was a lot higher.

Galiza warns that if someone were to look at the bank's data and not know there were different creatives and look at the audience as a whole, it would be easy to think that audience wasn't a good one to target. The reality is that when you don't control the test, you don't get the true narrative from the data.

Data only tells part of the story, it doesn't define the plot. And it can be taken to extremes, as Jim Mollica puts it: 'I do think that if you become too paralysed by the data inputs, it limits the potential of magic.' And the magic he refers to is the idea that seemingly comes from nowhere that makes the hair stand up on the back of our necks. We've all seen ads that move us, that make us think, 'I wish I'd had that idea', and this is the best our industry can offer. But if we live by the data alone, this won't happen.

Peter Field's view is that we need to 'be very wary of any metrics and any models that are served to you – always think like a human being. Be very wary that the media and digital bubbles in which we all live and operate in the real world are very different from the bubbles in which most marketers and business people live.'

Expecting creativity to survive on data alone doesn't give ideas the nutrition they need to develop. I wish I could find the podcast where a guest said that 'data is the shadows of people' because I'd like to attribute this brilliant quote to them. The quote sums up the problem with relying too heavily on data – if it's just the shadows that we are relying upon then we're not seeing reality.

Sutherland helps us entertain two views:

Creative people have always got the relationship wrong, and that's because they will naturally either, if they're acquiescent, okay, they'll either accept that creativity is the little bit of magic dust you add on the end. It's the icing on the cake, the cherry on the top, you know, it's the little thing you do, after all the serious, rational work has been done by the boring people. That's one take on creativity. The other take, which is a more aggressive one, is to see creativity in permanent opposition to rationality. And obviously that's kind of nonsense, because people being creative use rationality all the time as part of the creative process. And the two things should be actually deployed in parallel and seen as complementary, whereas instead, we either deploy them, apply them in series and see them as in opposition.

So it's all in the balance, rationality and creativity, data and ideas. Or as Gaunt puts it, 'Where it doesn't work is where you just think okay, the data is going to give me all the answers. So you really do need to get that balance right.'

Not adapting your approach to data over time

In Eskridge's experience the need for data changes as the brand evolves. When businesses start on their marketing journey the focus is on 'big splash type of campaigns'. In these stages brands are 'leaning more heavily on the creativity and not so much on the data'. She has observed that as a business matures after a launch they look to rein in the amount of spend on marketing.

It's not surprising to Eskridge that a lot of companies start off without measuring the marketing 'because they're trying to figure out what works'. She's observed companies trying every channel to see what's going to stick. Eventually organizations are realizing that they 'don't have time to put money or invest money in marketing that doesn't matter or it doesn't bring results'. This creates a pressure of having to scale the business faster with fewer resources. This calls for knowing what's working and what's not 'and so that's where the data comes into play'.

Ignoring intuition

Eskridge believes that there's a strong relationship with intuition and data, 'we possess this desire to actually lean heavily on what we can see' and data can create the illusion of being more truthful than it is. 'The reality of using only data is that you have blind spots and data, I could realistically create my own hypothesis out of some data. And it could be lacking, right, it could be lacking in contextual relevance and, you know, so many other things that go into interpreting that data.'

The key to bridging the gap between the truth and that data is intuition. For Eskridge, 'There's been times when I've looked at data, and... I know what it's telling me. But my intuition tells me that there's something else there. Where data is sourced from can lead you down the wrong path or tell you the story you want to be told, and not the truth.'

The important step here is to interrogate and ask 'why'? Or, as Hakan Yurdakul, puts it:

> I think data on an Excel is definitely useful. I mean, at least that means you're doing something, you're starting with something. Because a lot of companies don't even know the 'what'... they just use gut feel. And then one more level of advancement is they look at the data, but they just use diagnostic tools.

This helps brands see if 'my sales are going up, my sales are going down. I sell this much, that much. I am good in this city, this country, this group, fine, but they don't go down to why and how.' And that's what Yurdakul thinks the next level of interaction with your data should be, specifically, 'understanding the "why", going back to the root cause of things instead of just being reactive to your data'.

Are you Team Data or Team Creative – or both?

I blame the school system in the 1980s/90s (at least in the UK) for the way that Gen X today see themselves as being a creative person or not. If you can't be creative, then the only other route is to be organized. At school we were told we were no good at art or maths and were firmly nudged towards choosing a lane. You were loosely either a data person who dealt with facts or one of the make-it-up people. In reality most people are a mix of both. Even the most non-creative number nerd is able to have a conversation, dress themselves or choose something from a menu – all creative choices. And even the most wildly imaginative artist absorbs data through their five senses and makes predictions on what might happen next. As kids we were advised to pick lanes so we'd get better grades, not be more rounded and effective marketing people.

Anastasia Leng's view is:

I think the difficulty about these kinds of conversations is people are pitted
to choose one side. We take these highly complex issues like data-driven
creativity, and people feel compelled to say it's all data, creativity doesn't matter,
creativity will now be quantified or, you know, data will never be able to predict
everything creative. And the reality is, the answer is both are right. 'Paradox
mindset thinking' doesn't grab headlines. A paradox mindset is a mindset
that acknowledges that both of these things are true. And the difficulty is to
what extent? How do you navigate across the spectrum? These are not binary
questions. It's not data or creativity.

So it's not a choice to be either a data person or a creative person. Modern
marketing people need to be both to a degree. And one place where the
marriage of these two powers comes alive is performance marketing. Lisa
Calvino, Head of Digital Marketing at Brompton Bicycle, sees performance
marketing as the perfect balance between data and creativity. She told me:

Data backs up everything we do. It literally funds our budget. But without the
creative we're unable to do it. So we're unable to scale, to develop, to reach new
audiences, so they work hand in hand. Being able to scale up and talk about
one over the other is also a real benefit within the business. So for us, talking to
finance about extra budget, focusing solely on the numbers helps, but talking
to the marketing team about a potential campaign idea would really hammer
home the creatives that inspire and have worked really well. Obviously, I'm
biased, because it's my career, but I do believe that performance marketing
literally has the best of both worlds of being able to really tap into one or the
other, and ultimately, on a daily basis, within our team, we're a straight set of
the two. Our performance is only driven by how good our creative is, but we
can talk to both sides of the business.

The key here is that we can use data, not let it use us. Data is a support that
can be drawn upon to help us make better creative and media decisions –
let's not let data run wild, but use it as a data Robin to a creative Batman.

Note

1   Cherry, K (2020) Who Is Credited for the World's First Experimental
Psychology Lab? Verywell Mind, www.verywellmind.com/who-founded-the-
first-psychology-lab-2795250 (archived at https://perma.cc/V8C8-YLF8)

06

Mindset mastery: data meets creativity – part 2

'We can collect all of the data in the world, but why?'

TOM GROGAN

Faris Yakob shares the view that:

> Corporations, entities, nation states are unable to communicate with themselves
> in anything except numbers. So all qualitative data gets stripped out at lower
> levels, because it has to, because nothing is self-similar and fungible enough at
> the top level to make a comparison set across country-level data or corporation-
> level data except numbers, which means you turn everything into numbers.

And this proposes significant risks in how data is used by powerful groups,
including brands. His point is that 'big data is data that is so large you can't
work it out yourself; you need a machine to look at it'. And when a machine
is looking at it then everything becomes numerical. And when we look solely
at the numbers we can neglect the nuance.

Yakob recounts the tale from the Vietnam War when Robert McNamara
was drafted in from Ford to run the US's military campaign. He had a singular focus on one data point that would lead to victory if it was achieved.
This was a gruesome data point – the number of military casualties on the
enemy side. He was right in thinking that if this number increased, then
there would be a point where the war was won. This didn't take into account
a variety of other factors such as morale, media and politics, which played a
huge part.

Yakob notes that brands must understand the danger of measuring the
easiest thing to measure because this will likely not lead to measuring the

truth. It's human nature to measure what can easily be measured (probably clicks) and disregard what can't be easily measured or given a quantitative value. Worse than this is to presume what can't be measured isn't important, or, worse, think that if it can't be easily measured it doesn't exist.

It's easy to get lots of numerical data in advertising but we are in the business of people and in the business of emotion. When we are looking at a large number of people it's easy to collect clicks, views etc but because it's easy we can't confuse this with it being the most important data. Abundant data and important data aren't the same thing here.

Using data as a target

This is further confounded by the reality of Goodhart's law which states, 'When a measure becomes a target, it ceases to be a good measure'. When we come up with a target for our marketing we are giving ourselves and our teams (and suppliers) an incentive to game the system in order to get the reward. For example, if our goal is to double sales then we can flood the market with discounts and offers and crush profit (and a brand's premium position) in the process.

A tragic story of Goodhart's law in effect was when British officials in colonial India offered a bounty for cobra skins to try to curb the cobra population. This seemingly sensible plan came a cropper when Goodhart's law kicked in and some wily characters bred cobras for their skins. Once their game was discovered by the Brits, the cobra farmers released the snakes into the wild, which increased the population of cobras in the region.

Confusing interesting with insightful

Rosie and Faris Yakob are the founders of 'Genius Steals', which thrives on the idea that innovation is about mixing old ideas into new creations, not just copying. Faris and Rosie are globally recognized strategists and creatives who've lived and worked around the world for over nine years, bringing a nomadic edge to their work. I was lucky to get an hour with them on a call to get their take on data and creativity.

Rosie's antidote to Goodhart and McNamara is that 'You need a basket of data, looking to gather insight into what could help us make decisions about the next creative campaign'. Of course, all brands will have different-shaped baskets. The key here is to make sure that the data sets in your basket are going to help make better marketing decisions. Or, as Rosie puts it, 'Don't measure things unless they are going to help you make a decision. What decisions do we need to make and what data points will help us make those decisions?'

Don't confuse interesting with insightful. If your data tells you that your social ads have a better CTR than display ads, that may be interesting but it's not giving you any insight into the audience. This truth is also compounded by the fact that if brands are all using the same data points then we are likely to do the same things. If all brands are using aggregated data and advice from the advertising platforms then they will all do the same thing. For example, if 'best practice' is sending emails on a Tuesday then that's what everyone will do, which will instantly make Wednesday a better tactical choice for sending emails. Or, as Rosie puts it, 'If everyone has the same access to the data points, then we all do the same things.'

So assuming that you've got your basket of data, you're measuring the right things and staying clear of self-sabotaging McNamara fallacies, then it's your job to articulate data 'in a creative, interesting and inspiring way that will lead to more creativity down the line,' says Rosie.

But it's not over at this point for Rosie and Faris. The skill here is to use data and creativity in a convergent and divergent manner. This is the practice of going deep into the data and then 'zooming out' again. By nature, 'Planners compress and creatives lateralize', meaning that planners 'take on the burden of trying to turn data into insight and creatives make an attempt to make ideas that will solve the problem as best you know, as the strategy indicates, they should'.

The skill here is to be convergent in your thinking and dive into the data to find an insight when planning and then go broad and expansive when coming up with creative ideas. Or in other words, know 'when data is most useful within the process', according to Rosie, who argues that data is there to support creative thinking at the right time, not all the time.

One time data can count against brands is when they attempt to personalize. It's the Yakobs' view that personalizing ads to an individual or group of people isn't actually advertising. According to Faris, 'Personalization is basically always bad and nearly never a good idea of advertising' because part of the effect of advertising is that we all see the same thing. If we all get a different ad then we don't have a collective agreement on what that brand represents. At its worst they see Google and Meta's dynamic ad products as moving away from understanding the consumer, or in their words, 'We've sort of removed people from the process obviously a little bit.'

What data can't provide

At the time of writing, relying entirely on the data and letting the robots make the creative and media decisions leaves brands susceptible to the linear thinking of machines and will starve them of the unplanned and unpredictable brilliance of human thought.

This is a theme that runs through all of these interviews, that (numerical) data lacks the softness and empathy that is necessary to understand what a consumer thinks and feels. But we can't interview every possible human that might want to buy our product or service. Only an all-knowing deity would be able to do this, and perhaps be the ultimate market researcher. This kind of hire is probably off the cards for now.

So Faris Yakob's advice is, 'The idea of that data is to try and infer something about people you can use to get to the final point to make better marketing interventions of which some are media and some are creative.' For something to be creative there needs to be a leap or a new connection found between two things that is surprising and useful. If we are moronically following the data we'll be stumbling around in the dark.

As Alex Jenkins puts it:

> Okay, so we've all got kind of access to everything. Like the 'so what' bit I think suddenly ramps up as that's where the key advantages are, you know, at the moment. It may be that it's people who are just better at using ChatGPT, they're just fashioning more interesting prompts. They prompt and reprompt and reprompt in a way that extracts something out down the line – who knows what it's going to be, but it will for my money always be that just constantly looking at it from a different angle. There can be a point where creativity just dies.

I wish there was something more concrete than to say that sometimes you're just going to have to feel when you are too reliant on the data. Tom Goodwin tells us that we need to:

> … know when to use the data and when not to, know what decisions you're trying to make with the data. More data is not better data, better data is better data – know when to go with your heart and when to go with the data. Know when the data is wrong. You know, use your data generally to support decisions that you're making, rather than create the material in the first place.

It will take confidence to tell a data scientist they are wrong or that a data point is misleading or not useful. Tina Eskridge, who has found herself in this situation, says, 'There's been times when I've looked at data and I'm like, yeah, I know what it's telling me. But my intuition tells me that there's something else there.'

It's certainly not easy and this book aims to use the experience of those who have trodden this path before to help you make better marketing decisions. As Ceci Dones puts it, 'Anything that implies creativity, anything that implies growth, anything that implies transcendence, because change sucks. It's uncomfortable. And so by the very nature of their discomfort, that means we're on the right track with something.'

Angela Culver asks herself when she should believe the data versus leading with intuition. She believes both are very important in what we do:

> So it goes back to my skating. I would map out formulas on how to perfect my jumps. But, if I just did not feel 100 per cent that day, or I was not confident in landing my triple flip, I was not going to land it. Even though I did everything perfect by my spreadsheet, there was still a chance I would fall.
>
> And there were times where my intuition would say, this is not the jump for the day, even though you've landed this 100 times in practice, there would be something in my brain that just said, this is just not the one, and I would need to lean into my intuition versus leaning into the data. The balance is trying to figure out when you let one lead versus the other. I find in business, that can sometimes be hard... I don't think it's as hard for someone in the finance profession that is all numbers all the time, but when you're dealing with professions like marketing, it can be a struggle to make that determination.

Your intuition is the output of the unstructured data in your head. How are you going to use it?

Curiosity is the killer app

'Be positively curious... do not routinely accept data as fact.' – David Byrne

There's something reassuring about the idea of data. It can feel absolute, reliable and make us feel confident. If there's data to fall back on then this denotes that someone, somewhere has at least paid some attention and it's not a big guess. Data suggests some form of scientific rigour and sensibleness and therefore it must be a good thing. However, data in a marketing sense isn't all it's cracked up to be in Faris Yakob's mind. He told me, 'The voice of the consumer is not statistical inferences of large datasets, the voice of the consumer is what real people are feeling and thinking in the world.' So we need to have an interest to go beyond what the numbers are telling us.

During my research one point stopped me in my tracks. Rosie Yakob said, 'Either you are inherently curious or you are not.' In all of my discussions for this book I'd not had a moment of clarity like this one. Many of the insights shared in my research helped me see the bigger picture but this point felt important.

If you're not curious you can't be creative. If you ask, 'What will happen if I draw this line, write this word, sing this note, move this way, add this point, change this idea?' then you are being curious and acting on that thought makes you creative. An important part of being creative is being curious about what could be and then seeing what happens when you do that thing.

Equally, on the data side, if you're not curious about what's in the data then you're unlikely to find an insight that will inspire creativity. Collecting data for the sake of it is miserly, it has no value without getting into the data and finding meaning behind it. If an unusual read from the data doesn't make you ask 'why?' then you're going to be up against it to make data and creativity work. In short, if you want to get data and creativity to sing in harmony you're going to have a curious mindset, or at the very least be curious as to why you don't. Without curiosity you're unlikely to find anything interesting in your data and without it you're reducing the chances of your creativity standing out. A curious mindset will set you up for success with data, creativity and ads.

Jon Williams told me, 'Every creative has a curious mind, and all of the best ideas come out of asking, why? Why does it have to be like that? Why can't it be different? Why do you do it like that? Why do you do that? We take for granted so many things that we do in this business.'

I've worked in marketing for 17 years and the most consistent phrase I've heard in this time is 'it's changing so quickly' but said as if that's something new and offers some guidance. It doesn't – change in advertising tech is always happening. The nature of market competition means that someone somewhere is always trying to oust the incumbent with something new. And the marketing publishing industry loves something new – its entire trade media depends on it. We're fixated by shiny new objects and distracted by trends while the basics of marketing don't change that fast. We're all deluged with demands on our eyeballs for the new thing that's going to make our marketing lives easier and quicker.

One solution to the relentless downpour of things to click on comes from Jess Burley. She never leaves something to read later. If she sees something new, then she dives right in:

> Actually, don't leave it till later to go back and read it because you'll never get back to it. Actually read it, right now. And even if you only skim-read it you'll have picked up enough knowledge that actually when you then are faced with

something that requires you to know about that thing, you at least know about it, and then you can go back and do the deep dive and understand it. But if you don't even know about it, how do you know to even go and look for it? So my advice is don't leave learning for later, learn it now.

So we need to be curious at speed. Don't wait for a good time – expose yourself to what hidden goodness might be inside the data and the different ways the data might come to you. Of course balance is also needed. It's not enough to be data savvy and curiously creative; you need to be able to flex between the two with ease. As Lex Bradshaw-Zanger puts it, 'There are days when I love the creativity and innovation and there are days when I'm very, very data-centric and factual.' This needs to be the default setting of the modern marketer.

One of the most difficult lessons to learn at the start of Automated Creative was that although we'd invented a technology to help brands understand which elements of their ads drove the outcomes they needed, we weren't that good at spotting which ads would work the best ourselves. All of our years working for creative and digital agencies prior hadn't given us the gift to be able to predict which ad would work when multiple creatives ran and were optimized over time based on the data.

Thankfully we were not alone and we soon realized that the inability to pick which ad would win from a large number of creatives was uniform. Adam Wright has a similar perspective:

> Even with years of experience, creative and customer behaviour always surprises me. And I think that's when I realized that the best creative in the world, and what you think is the best creative in the world, and even with the smartest minds in the world, actually, your kind of win rates for those the majority of the time are very, very small. And I became pretty fascinated with, like, how we could work basically with the team's ability to be able to predict whether or not things would win and it mainly boils down to how bad I was at being able to predict winners.

So we need to accept that we are not right as often as we think we are. We need to stay curious and be quick to take on new ideas, and change between analytical and creative mindsets easily.

When to trust your gut over data

Culver shares a story that highlights the balance between data-driven decision making and intuition. A tenacious colleague insisted on hosting a product launch event in New York City in mid-July. The historical data suggested attendance would be low due to remote working behaviour. Culver was sceptical and told her colleague, 'You get the people there, and my team will support it 100 per cent.' Against the odds, the event exceeded expectations, drawing 200 attendees instead of the predicted 25.

Culver notes that while data provides valuable guidance, there are moments when taking a calculated risk driven by the passion and determination of an individual can yield unexpected success: 'If I had followed the data, we wouldn't have had the event,' she admits. However, her decision factored in both the data and her gut feeling about the individual's ability to deliver.

She emphasizes the importance of curiosity in working with data, likening it to a child repeatedly asking 'why?' Effective decision making requires not just analysing numbers but continuously questioning assumptions, considering alternative paths and being open to pivoting based on real-world insights. While intuition is harder to quantify than structured data, it plays a crucial role in decision making.

How much data do you need?

There are thousands of ad tech companies who are all trying to win clients, grow those clients' accounts and sell their businesses to bigger companies so they can retire on a yacht somewhere. That's the ad tech start-up game – you're either in it or fuelling it. There's nothing wrong with that but the common currency of most of those ad tech companies is data, tonnes of the stuff. For every digital action that happens there is a server blinking in an air-conditioned room processing that moment into data. That data will seep into spreadsheets, dashboards and decks. It will eventually wash up like a tiny grain of sand onto a beach with countless billions of other data points that the marketer needs to make sense of. And this starry sky of infinite data points contrasts with another data set – our own lived experience.

We have more data than just the numbers

Tiffany Rolfe says:

> When you think about what we do as creative people, we're actually using data. It's just what I think of as a very limited data set. And those are our gut and

our instincts, our data. It's just our own really small set of data from our own personal experiences and the work experiences we've had and that obviously our data increases the more senior a person we are.

Goodwin takes this one step further:

I think we should come to all of these conversations with the presumption that we're good at what we do, and our gut is normally right, because otherwise we wouldn't be in this industry. And that's not arrogance… we need to accept the reality, which is that we have way more data in our hands than we realize we do.'

What data is useful? What isn't?

Jenkins' view is:

So even basic stuff, like how are we going to improve our click-through rates? How are we going to improve open rates, how are we going to get our social following up? You can take action on anything you're monitoring, right? So if you've got the wrong sort of data, you're probably spending hours looking at dashboards and reports and doing nothing about anything you're learning. It's just an observation of stuff that's happened. If you've got too much data, ironically, it probably feels the same. You've got loads and loads of stuff. But there's probably a huge amount of wastage of stuff. You're not doing data you're not doing anything with.

The amount of data creates a huge problem. It's hard for a marketer to know which data is useful and which data isn't. Wright told me:

I think probably everyone has marketeers and particularly anyone who's interested in the kind of data side and performance side of marketing will get this on a daily basis, that they are overwhelmed. They find they've got too much data. My personal experience with data overwhelm is that it's kind of a combination of having too much data but mainly an inability to sift through the noise to find those meaningful insights. Nothing is going to replace human-like creativity and the kind of understanding and thinking about that, but if you've got the power of AI to find patterns and insights [it can] help you to dig through that in a quicker way and stop you from being overwhelmed.

Find something that works for you.

Despite the volume of data available, Lisa Calvino says:

I think no one's ever gonna feel like they've got enough… as long as you're really clear with what action you are trying to get out of it, I don't think you need heaps and heaps of data. You just need to be able to know where to look and at what points you are able to take an action from it.

One solution to the volume problem comes from Wright:

> I think there's always going to be a lot of intangible things that you can't quantify or kind of digest down and distil down into a specific formula. And I think, to be successful in our types of roles and in our types of business, I think you have to be good with that harmony. I think otherwise it's going to drive you utterly insane, like trying to measure everything and try and figure it all out and what makes humans work and a lot of the time like you genuinely don't know – it's just if you find something that works and you double down on it.

This last bit of advice chimes for me and it's a simple question to ask: do we have data that helps us guide creativity that works and is actually effective? If you can prove that then, as Wright says, doubling down is the way to go. Overwhelm means you're overloaded with data that isn't delivering results. Which data sets can you ditch that won't affect your creative output?

Who is your data serving? You, or the supplier of the data?

Getting your hands on data is easy, but the skill is learning to know what to ignore and what is truly telling you what you need to know. It's important to always understand the motivation of the person who is supplying you with the data. Is their motivation aligned with yours or are they inflating the value of their data because it suits their agenda?

Sam Gaunt's take is:

> A brand needs to take responsibility for itself to understand what's out there because as we all know, agencies have got other commercial interests – they might have their own preferred partners, got their own commercial arrangements and so on. So that's a great starting point.
>
> You can certainly learn some stuff, but you also need to be open minded to what else is out there because there's a whole load of start-ups as well… offering new ways of doing things. And the brands that will win are the ones which are open minded and are exploring what's out there, and testing things as well.
>
> That's, you know, the most valuable data for me is data, which is, kind of, it's unbiased, and it's completely agnostic of, you know, where the who's overseeing the data or who owns the data is kind of irrelevant. The data is just what it is. It just shows what people are, what people are actually doing out there in the real world. And that's what's really powerful for brands because without that kind of

data, you're going back to the days when you've got, you know, you've only got qualitative data and you've only got what people are telling you that they're doing.

Data can fill in the blanks

Meredith Herman isn't alone in thinking that the amount of data available to marketers 'can be overwhelming'. The example she gives is when it comes to getting people to switch to Sensodyne from their competitors. The cost of getting someone to switch to Sensodyne is a 'big factor' and just looking at the data around this cost doesn't tell the whole story. Haleon know they can get people to switch, but that can be incredibly expensive. The key for Herman is to get to grips with the reality of Sensodyne's brand equity versus competitors. Her point is that data helps us improve our understanding of the consumer and by using data we can better fill in those blanks around barriers to connecting with them.

Going outside/beyond the data you have

A key mindset is to think outside the data that you have. Data isn't an accurate reflection of the world; it's lots of records of things that happened somewhere at some point. It's imperfect, even if you are lucky enough to have the right data in the first place. So marketers should always be on the lookout for new and better data that might help them understand their target market better. More data for the sake of it just takes up time, so we need to be thinking about how data can help us understand our customers better. What can data reveal that we didn't know before, what new usable truths will it uncover? Being curious about new data sets that help us know our targets better and inspire more effective marketing is what we are after. We're not after more data; having data is a means and not an end. Always ask, 'What do we want to know that we don't know now that we wish we did?' – and sniff out the data that will tell us that. Being open to new ideas and inspiration will make our teams stronger.

Rolfe puts this simply: 'We give more value to things we can quantify when actually the most valuable things are unquantifiable.' The idea that data we can't collect is the most valuable to the creative process is challenging for the data-driven marketer.

Rory Sutherland reveals a little about his internal process, or lack of it:

I say this to clients occasionally, I say 'I'll let you into a secret'. Okay, we pretend we have a process... we need a process, because you've got to start somewhere. We also need to pretend there's a process, because otherwise, procurement will say, well, we're not going to give you a load of money just to go off at random. Once authorized, I produced really good work following the process. More often than not, your best work comes from a deviation from the process, or from a very messy process, or in extreme cases, what I call a 'process of no process', where you sit around talking and then someone gets lucky. If you want to grow and if you want resilience as an organization, or, for that matter, as an organism, you need something more, which is, you need to be able to adapt. You need to be resilient, to change, and you need to grow. And you're not going to grow simply by sitting around and only taking advantage of opportunities that, you know, that are readily to hand.

An effective process is a fine thing, but the magic may lurk just slightly beyond what is known and what is planned for.

How to use data

The industry is awash with reports from big platforms and aggregated data sets that tell us what the trends and best practices are. This kind of data is convenient for you as a marketer to get, but it's also convenient for your competitors to get as well. So by getting your hands on that data you're only ruling out the lazy competitors who can't be bothered to get it as well, let alone act on it. The real skill is to get your own data that your competition doesn't have, the right data, and have the correct attitude and skills for making the most of it.

But not all brands have the resources to create unique, structured and useful data. Others need to be creative with the data they get and how they use it. As Dones puts it, 'Are we reinventing something that already exists? Just because we want to label it as unique. It doesn't have to be unique. You just need to apply it better than anybody else.'

Make a hypothesis

Let's assume you can get your hands on some data, be that your own or someone else's or a mix of both. You need to make a plan for what to do with it that is going to result in more effective marketing. Gaunt tells us:

It's really critical that to get the right creative ideas… it (data) has to be organized in the right way and it has to be user friendly. And it has to be able to answer questions, right? You need to be able to ask questions of data and to get the answer from it. Because data on its own isn't going to answer any questions unless you are, you know, asking something of it. You need to have a hypothesis that it can help to disprove or to prove.

Having the right hypothesis is a great place to start. What do you want to know about the audience that you don't currently know that data might be able to tell you? Proving a hypothesis is a great way to work out if the data that you have is going to help you be more creative. You can ask yourself, 'Does the data I have prove or disprove my hypothesis about the audience?' If your answer is, 'I don't have a hypothesis' – then your data is a mess and you're collecting it in the hope that the answer will reveal itself by some small miracle.

The best process is to let creative and data work together in partnership. As Dones tells us:

> I use both in an iterative, continuous and dynamic kind of way. I consider both tools almost like a partnered dance. To create a beautiful dance, I need both working in partnership where depending on the specific task in the process one tool may lead the other and vice versa.

If your data doesn't prove or disprove your hypothesis then it isn't set up the right way. Gaunt's view is that you should 'let the data do the thinking that you need to do. Always ask why you're seeing what you're seeing in the data, and why is it valuable.'

The mindset of asking yourself why you are seeing what you are seeing is the key skill here. It's not productive to look at the data and repeat it back to your organization at face value. Cutting and pasting a graph into a deck without further investigation isn't going to lead to new levels of creativity. But using that data to ask the next question and to peel back the next layer is the path to unlocking the knowledge that will lead to more effective work. Or, as Jenkins puts it, 'You're generating reports, checking dashboards, that sort of thing. But fundamentally, data is just a way of knowing what is going on. Okay, great. So you know what's going on, but the killer question is, what are you going to do about it?'

We need to remember the purpose of using data in the first place. The purpose of using data is to make more effective marketing, or as Jon Willams simply puts it, 'Data will inform a brief, and a well-informed brief creates the best work.'

The role of data is to support but not define the creative. It's a tool to make humans a bit better. Burley tells us:

> So far everything that you've seen does not somehow do away with the need for human intervention or intelligence in the way that marketers work because ultimately, what our job has always been is to synthesize what we understand about the consumer that we're trying to talk to, or the brand, the product that we're trying to put in front of them or the message that we're trying to put in front of them. And actually, what we do with these tools, therefore, is to accelerate our ability to absorb a lot of information fast in order to be able to come to our conclusion, and there still has to be a recommendation, a piece of work, a master asset. And actually it doesn't do away with any of that. What it does is it just aids it and helps it.

Generate meaningful insights

Herman leads global marketing services at Haleon. Her journey to getting there is a really interesting one. She started investment banking on Wall Street and was 'terrible'. She then pivoted towards marketing, admitting she liked the story more than she liked the numbers. She then spent 15 years at different creative agencies as an account person and then went over to GSK, now Haleon, for the past 10 years. In the reception of the Haleon offices in Warren, New Jersey, where I interviewed Herman, was a giant screen displaying their stock price compared with their closest competitors, which was in the least a symbolic nod to the power of live data and its importance to the business.

Herman's agency pedigree and exposure to brand-side data puts her in a rare position. She's seen the hustle and fluidity of agency life while navigating vast corporate architecture. The diversity of challenges she deals with in uniting creativity and data is something she relishes. Her approach to finding the balance of these two forces is collaboration. When it comes to data, Herman's view is:

> There's executional-level work and then there's more strategic positioning work. So when I think of the qualitative information, a lot of times we're using that to make sure that we're headed in the right direction, and then you're quantifying that direction with quant to make sure that the depth is there.

This is an elegant way of successfully utilizing the extensive gallery of dashboards and sea of spreadsheets available to her. Knowing when and where to use data is an important skill in making effective creative.

Be a first mover, but always check your data

The good news is that with a data-driven mindset you don't need to make big bets with your marketing. You can de-risk by leveraging tech to test and learn.
As Dones told me:

As a data person and a researcher, I'm always keen to try new technologies in a sandbox. De-risk and run an experiment. Have a learning agenda that's focused on consumer value. Use that information to determine when AI will help to amplify and accelerate and when intuitive intelligence is more important for creating the 'big idea'.

One of the challenges that marketers face with data and creativity is that all the platforms are selling the same thing to everyone. Wright's advice is:

If you carry on listening to the next new shiny thing and what the platforms tell you, then inevitably you're going to be chasing your tail because they're going to be out there telling every single agency and every single brand to go and do what they want them to go and do versus, kind of, being governed the other way. So use some of your test budget to go and try it but equally listen to the data to then say, is that actually working or not? In a nutshell, you are constantly learning and unlearning anyway.

The trick here is to work out if the new thing works for your brand. It may work brilliantly for everyone who tried it first and got first-mover advantage but in reality we're looking for sustainably effective marketing. And a strategy that is based on doing the new things that the platforms sell us is going to be hit and miss. The question to ask yourself is, 'Is my team set up to test quickly and report back without disrupting the main job to be done?'
Gaunt adds:

So for me, it is very simple, it's experimentation that uses data to understand the impact of new ideas and innovation... If you've got no existing data, it doesn't restrict new ideas from forming. It just means that you've got that culture of experimentation, that you've got the tools in place and the analytics in place to help you collect the data to help you understand if it's working or not.

Be agile, be open

You should be getting your teams 'comfortable with being uncomfortable', says Calvino:

Something that works today might not work tomorrow, and there's no rhyme or reason for that. It's just the world is changing at such a fast pace. Something that was funny yesterday might be offensive today or vice versa. And so you just need to be able to kind of pivot and be as transparent as possible.

She continues, 'It's okay to fail, but shout about it and learn from it as quickly as possible. And people will respect and trust you more from this.' Calvino thinks that 'trying to hide something or say something worked or trying to make out that it worked when it didn't – is really telling.'

Calvino told me that the older you get and the more experience you gain, 'you can really see when that's happening. If it isn't, just say it isn't.' This gives teams the chance to change, amend and learn.

She also encourages us to:

> Just be bold and test things out of the box. I think it's easy to get caught up in doing the same things… be constantly looking for the next thing to test and that thing doesn't have to come from data. So for example TikTok, how do you know that that's going to work and how will you know what works on it unless you try it?

Where data is most powerful

By now hopefully you're realizing that data isn't an all-powerful force and doesn't solve all marketing problems and won't give you a solution all tied up neatly in a bow. As Jenkins tells us, 'Data is fundamentally a rearview mirror. It tells us what has already happened or, at best, what's happening now.' And what is happening now is a hugely underused source of data. If you understand how your ads are being reacted to live then if you have the systems in place you can change those ads accordingly.

Goodwin's view is, 'There are two very interesting ways to think about data and one is data that is used almost at the start of the process to inform what you do. And then data that's used at the end of the process to justify and to celebrate, and to optimize what you do.'

Different data for different stages

All too often brands are seeing awareness, consideration and performance ads as wholly distinct ads with no impact on each other. Quite often these come from different departments. I've met brand teams who sit in different offices and have totally different incentives to performance teams who are meant to bring home the bacon. Let's not even start on how detached the .com/website or CRM teams can be. Let's assume for now these teams all work in harmony and communication is working, the idea that the different stages of the funnel act independently is wrong.

How likely are you to click on an ad for a product you've never heard of from a company you never knew existed and go to a website and purchase something there and then that costs more than a few pounds or dollars? I am 100 per cent sure that this has happened, but it is incredibly rare and so much so that no marketer in their right mind would bet their marketing budget on this happening that often.

The reality is that all awareness, consideration and conversion ads do each other's jobs in an unpredictable and messy way. A successful performance ad benefits hugely from the awareness and consideration ads that preceded it. As Peter Field put it, 'The argument of *The Long and the Short of it* is to say that there are two sides to effectiveness: long term – the brand and short term – performance. You have to do both and you have to do both in some kind of balance.'

The exact balance is hard to pin down and will be different for all marketers. And data is there to help and to be used in different ways as you convert your prospects into customers.

Seeing the human in the data

'What's effective has been around for centuries; the basics of human behaviour don't really change that much.' – Barbara Galiza

In this chapter we've talked about having too much, too little or the wrong sort of data. Even if we have the right data and are using it in the right way, it can send us down a complex and twisting rabbit warren of data dead ends. And leave us wondering how we got into it in the first place. At some point we need to stop and remind ourselves that marketing is a communication tool, and that we are speaking to humans and not spreadsheets. As Field puts it, 'We're not talking about machines. We're not talking about computers. We're not talking about the world of rational, logical decision making. We're talking about how human beings make decisions and that is absolutely not logical and absolutely not rational.'

It's ok to accept that chaos and unmeasurable events play a part in what we do. But the promise of data-driven marketing is that we can do better than gut feel and random chance. Data can make us better creatives but not replace our creativity. Anastasia Leng's view is:

> I do not believe data will ever replace the role of a creative director, nor do I believe that data will ever be able to do everything that a creative director does. On the other hand, on the creative side, people can acknowledge that there are areas where data helps us shape and make better decisions about the creative roads to pursue. It could be an amplifier, it could be something that gives us more conviction that this is a direction that consumers embrace.

So data can be an enabler, can help us innovate and generate new ideas. I'm part of a business where we use data to unlock the hidden secrets of why a brand's ads work. However, this can be done in the wrong way. If too much emphasis is put on the data alone then we are back in a mist of unusable data signals.

Matt Cosad told me about a time at an FMCG brand where they were too focused on the data: 'What we were finding was we were optimizing for "engagement" and making assumptions about the different aspects of a piece of content that were driving those clicks and just getting things completely wrong.'

Cosad has been experimenting with 'computer vision to assess different aspects of creative, like when the humans appear (in the ad), what facial expressions they have, what colour palettes we're using'. He notes that 'You start to be able to quantify more and more which aspects of an ad are correlated to creative performance.' This sounds incredible! However it wasn't necessarily a good thing. As Cosad puts it, 'Every time you dig deeper and deeper down, I realized that micromanaging the tactics within creative production was never producing as impactful creative as focusing on delivering a good story in an engaging way.

This is the perfect story of when letting the data steer the ship doesn't work. Data is a compass and not a map. Human creativity enhanced by data is the way forward.

Cosad remembers:

> That really was for me, the 'aha' moment… we were looking numerically at creative and trying to boil it down into a set of numbers. And then tweak those numbers to produce the best-performing creative but it was never performing as well as if we started with a better creative idea in the first place.

This story shows that if we only follow the numerical data we can refine an idea but the real skill is to use the data to unearth new creative possibilities that make better ads overall. We must remember that we're trying to create emotion in our audiences, trying to make them feel positive thoughts about our brands so at the point of purchase, they choose the brands we represent. So we need to make the data work for us and that means unlocking new and innovative creative ideas and not repeating nuanced versions of the past.

Winning battles with data (with senior management)

I'm no expert in navigating large corporation politics but when I quizzed Jim Sterne on why aligning data with creativity didn't always happen he gave an insightful perspective. He told me, 'If everything's going well, the marketing department has the power baton... you can spend the money... you can run a big advertising campaign because we're doing well. We're hitting our stakeholder stock price value so great, spend some more money!' But if the brand's favour takes a downturn, then 'The power baton goes over to sales – now we need revenue. And then, if they're not doing well the power baton goes to the CFO. It's all about cutting costs.'

Sterne's view is that it all comes down to who has the power in the moment to say 'no'. This ability to torpedo data-centric marketing is being overlooked. A typical conversation in Sterne's view might go like this:

> We're going to do this campaign. We're going to put all this work together. It's going to cost a lot of money. Everybody thinks it's great. And somebody we didn't see coming from operations or human resources or the legal department says, oh, 'we can't do this because...' and the whole thing is scrapped. Nobody knew that they had the power to say 'no'.

Sterne's view is that getting data and creativity moving will come down to 'Who has the ear of the authority, who has influence without status? Who can just derail the whole thing?'

As Calvino puts it:

> I think what's really challenging is if you have senior stakeholders... that feel very passionately about something, and you can't disprove it from data because I think that they will have that opinion for whatever reason, and it could be really valid or it could be totally invalid, but if you can't prove it or disprove it, you kind of have to go along with it. And I think that that's where it's really messy.

The irony here is that if you have data to prove your position then creating an argument for more data becomes easier.

Herman has done this successfully by placing a focus on getting the foundations of a business-wide data strategy in place. She's set up systems to track media spend and how much is spent on creative production and adaptation at a brand and campaign level. Her data gives her transparency on how many campaigns are running and how many assets. Crucially this isn't about creating a volume of data but to 'help us focus' by joining up the underlying data to make new logical choices. This is exciting for Herman as her team helps her 'illuminate what are the biggest problems we need to tackle… having that data is the first step.' She concedes this is foundational work. But marketing isn't a race to be the first, but to be the best. Herman says, 'It all starts with that underlying data and it being organized so that you can make sense of it. So I find it exciting.' This commitment to getting the right data to solve the right problem is the best foundation that creative can have. Brands should take inspiration from this attitude: 'We're just at that point of seeing the glaring problems that we need to now solve.'

Winning battles with partners

The challenge doesn't just stop internally; being right is not enough. When you go to market, there are more battles to be won.

Sinem Kaynak shared an intriguing story with me. Her team had developed a new product concept using AI, which was then validated through surveys with humans. They presented this AI-generated idea to their marketing team in North America, expecting immediate addition to the innovation funnel. However, they encountered unexpected resistance. The team hesitated to share the idea with the retailers, preferring to stick closer to the brand's established offerings. They suggested considering the AI-inspired product for a future date, two years down the line.

This response was a source of frustration for Kaynak, who saw it as a clear instance of personal bias overriding data-driven decisions. Despite the AI's backing by millions of data points and alignment with consumer preferences, the team's decision makers trusted their intuition over the AI's recommendations. This clash between the team's desires and the innovative, data-supported product highlighted the challenges of overcoming human bias. Kaynak's story emphasizes the importance of data over intuition in decision making, showcasing how reliance on personal bias can overlook the potential unlocked by unbiased, AI-generated insights. Interestingly, it was only when the retailers came back asking for similar products to what was recommended by AI analysis that the team decided to reconsider the project.

There's always more work to be done with data and creativity. And some of the best in the industry take that work home.

Cosad told me, 'The other thing that I found really transformational is working on personal projects in my private life; from a creative perspective that really made me think about what's going on in my day job.'

Impressively, Cosad has 'been trying to create a short animated TV series using generative AI and really starting to understand its limitations.' He is learning about how Gen AI 'fails to produce exactly what you want and how you need to work with the tools.' His approach has given him an understanding of what can and can't be done with these technologies.

Cosad told me that his out-of-hours research 'has produced some pretty hilarious conversations with creative agencies who are trying to sell us customized large language models for a huge amount of money. When in reality I've already done this in my bedroom like a few nights before.'

Cosad concedes:

> It sounds kind of basic but using being creative in your personal life and using the creative technologies that are available to us now for your own personal projects has been invaluable for me in terms of making sure that I understand what is going on from a creative production perspective in the industry. It's really important.

Summary

As marketing practitioners we are going to continue to be bombarded with new forms of data and demands for more effective creativity to be delivered at an ever-increasing scale and it will all have to work. So getting our heads in the right place to begin with will be a huge advantage and allow us to see past the shiny new objects and look for the truth that will get us closer to our customers.

Marketing will continue to be a problem, not a puzzle, for many years to come and asking the right questions about the business problem is the first step – not getting out the advertising hammers in search of nails. The less boring our products and positioning are, the less advertising will have to do for us. But once we are on the road of paying to interrupt our customers then we need to use data as a compass and not a map; to some that will be scary but that data can take us to new places.

We must resist the temptation to use data to cover our backsides and aim for a creative lowland where we will be aiming to not lose and ultimately never win. Data can inform our creativity but not constrain it and we don't need to pick a side – the reality is you're already on team data and team creativity.

The easiest thing to measure and the truth are not likely to be the same thing; you're going to need a basket of data to make sure you've got insight and are not stuck in the trap of being just interesting. And even if your creativity is data led, it doesn't mean it's good. It's tough, but now that you have read this chapter you have absorbed many years of experience from successful data-guided marketers who know that best practice is common practice, and you're better than that.

In short, let's be data guided and not data driven. Data works for us, and not the other way around.

KEY TAKEAWAYS

- Look beyond aggregate advice and create your own data.
- Use data to navigate and not dictate your creativity.
- Always know what you're aiming for: brand love, more revenue or lower costs.

07

Assembling the dream team

Given you've got this far I'm going to assume you're committed to using data and creative effectively but unless you're on your own you're going to need a team to work with you. But building a team can be tricky – here's exactly how to get it right.

The good news is that you can get the right balance of creative and data skills to work. David Byrne gave McDonald's UK as a 'close to perfect' example of creating this balance. Their ad agency, Leo Burnett, had managed to collect 'excellent' sales data on menu seasonality over the course of 50 months. Byrne told me:

> The McDonald's marketing team had excellent sales data on menu seasonality,
> their media channel performance and softer, more instinctive knowledge
> on their creative performance. This almost sounds too good to be true,
> but they somehow managed to make sure their agency briefs were always
> complementary, taking learnings from previous campaigns to inform them so
> there was incremental performance each season. Because of the mutual trust and
> healthy tension between the McDonald's clients and the Leo Burnett team, there
> was always room for creativity and continuity, 'a perfect balance'.

I wish I could say this is common, but my research and experience proved that, sadly, the opposite is true. This was highlighted to me in the commonly referenced '5 Monkeys' fable shared with me by godfather of digital analytics Jim Sterne. A short summary of the fable is that there is a room with five monkeys, a ladder and a banana hanging over the top of the ladder. The first monkey runs up the ladder in an attempt to grab the banana and then the people running this theoretical experiment spray the monkey with water from a fire hose. Then the next monkey goes up the ladder and proceeds to get sprayed with the hose too and so on with each of the five monkeys. As a result of this, all the monkeys learn that they don't want to go up the ladder anymore because they will be soaked in water. Next, the people running the hypothetical experiment rotate out one of the monkeys with a new one; as it sees the banana and attempts to reach for the ladder, the now wet monkeys will prevent the new monkey from climbing up the ladder. Over time, as each of the old monkeys is replaced with a new one until none of the original set of monkeys remain, none of the new monkeys will attempt to take the banana. None of them have directly been sprayed with the fire hose, *but* they all collectively know it's a bad idea to take the banana.[1]

You need to avoid this situation when it comes to data, creativity and marketing. Fire hoses, real or hypothetical, aren't going to cut it. Sterne's view is that the fire hose in most companies is a process. An outdated process put in place once upon a time because something didn't work. Unless your process was built around data, creativity and ads, things must change and that comes from the top.

Effective data usage starts with leadership

The way to avoid giving your staff the fire hose experience is for the CMO *or* most senior marketing person to communicate what role data plays in the organization. As Sam Gaunt puts it:

> The Chief Marketing Officer needs to have the ability to articulate a clear vision around the role of data within a marketing organization to help drive marketing forward. That then needs to filter down through the organization so everyone can understand what they could be doing with the data and what they're expected to do with the data.

When you're infusing data with creativity it can't be a department or 'someone else's job'. It needs to be part of the culture of how the marketing department works. Just whacking some graphs in a quarterly report isn't going to change anything. The power of data can only be unlocked when the leadership shows why and how this should be done.

The importance of championing success and learning from failures

Global Marketing and Strategy Executive, Tina Eskridge, has led large teams in the ad tech space and believes the way to deliver data and creativity successfully together is to create the culture you want. The culture Eskridge develops in her team is based around engagement, vulnerability in sharing ideas and fostering freedom: 'That's where the true creativity comes from.'

Eskridge accepts that it can be tough to incorporate these elements into every team. On the first day of leading a team, she says, you think, 'Can they do the job?' Standardly, the team will most likely be thinking, 'Can you do the job?' The first step is making sure the team has some common ground and asking them, 'What's important to you?' It's Eskridge's experience that most people will find they have more things in common than they don't and once you find that they have this common bond, you start to cultivate trust.

Once trust has been established then Eskridge gets her team to make sure to highlight their successes and their failures: 'That's where trust and freedom kicks in. As you highlight failure, I think people start to realize that they can think outside the box.'

When this works well teams start to get new foundational experiences where everybody is putting their best foot forward. By doing this they're surpassing simple experimentation and instead they're thoughtfully collecting data and leveraging instinct. When this is done well, Eskridge says it is beautiful, 'like a symphony'.

But this hasn't always been the case in Eskridge's teams. When reflecting on one of her past teams she realized they didn't measure a lot of their marketing: 'The team was afraid to measure because they didn't want to know if it wasn't working.' The team worried that if the business knew the marketing wasn't working then budgets would be taken away and their performance would be judged.

Eskridge wasn't fazed by this: 'You win some, you lose some. Some campaigns do quite well and others are not so exceptional.' Her approach was to look at the data and find out how to measure what matters – 'dig into the why'. Then she advises to create a feedback loop where the team goes back and tests something different.

To harness data and creativity effectively, Eskridge aims to create a mindset where her teams are competing against themselves: 'You're competing against your greatest effort to date and you want to go back and repeat that cycle over and over and over again.' This process of testing and learning allows her brands to grow: 'Tiny incremental changes matter. It's the little tweaks that we do that make a campaign more impactful.'

Constructing an effective creative team

When it comes to building a data-fuelled creative team, Eskridge is on the hunt for someone who doesn't fit a template. She's seeking diversity of thought: 'I really look for people who want to challenge the ways in which we've been doing things.' The core skills she looks for are storytelling with data, adding value through diversity of thought and using data to make creative decisions.

In Eskridge's view, what you do with data is just as important as how you do it. This, in part, is down to fun. Using data and creativity together to encourage experimentation with her teams is only possible in a culture of trust and joyful curiosity is a necessary part of that. She loves to ask the question, 'How can I blow this out of the water and do something even more creative and cutting-edge while improving results along the way?'

Eskridge encourages us to find the right data that lets us see the whole customer in the world they inhabit, then use this insight to inspire creativity in an atmosphere of trust and fun. 'As a leader make sure that people know data is not meant to be a restriction. Instead use data for insight and as a guidepost. In order to foster growth you must have creativity with data and the perspective of what data enables.'

What role does data play in your marketing organization?

Culture is one thing, but using data effectively needs a plan. Gaunt tells us that senior leadership needs to give the team a clear articulation of the role data plays and a data strategy: 'Any strategy is about organization of resources to deliver against an objective.' He insists that we need to know how we are organizing our data resources and if we are collecting the right data: 'What are we doing with the data that we are collecting? What other data could we be collecting? How is it all brought together?'

It's clearly more complicated than having a dashboard or two. Ask yourself:

- What role does data play in your organization?
- Is data going to be used to better understand your customer so you can communicate with them in their language?
- Is data going to be used to cut costs?
- Is data going to be used to track the competition's creative output?
- Is data going to help you develop new products?

The list goes on and on.

The brand's leadership should feel like the brand is evolving in ways that improve its relevance and its connection to its consumers. There should be meaningful insight from data to understand consumers better. Gaunt says:

Alarm bells should be ringing if that's not happening, because it means that they're either collecting a whole load of data no one's looking at, they're not collecting the right data in the first place, the right people are not in the right roles to use that data properly, *or* they don't have the right culture to encourage that kind of observation to generate insight.

Your teams need to be focused on delivering actionable insight from your data. If your habits do not change as a result of analysing your data then it won't work for your team, it will just take up your time and work against you.

Creating a feedback loop

To build a team that combines data and creativity, Head of Digital Marketing at Brompton Bicycles Ltd, Lisa Calvino, emphasizes the delicate balance of assembling both creative and logical thinkers: 'You need a combination of creative and logical thinkers within the team, because both those traits are tricky to teach. It's really key to find a balance of team members who are naturally passionate about both.' She recognizes that individuals often have innate strengths in either creativity or analysis, and these differences help the team even each other out. Calvino has worked with both analytical and creative marketeers but the true advantage comes from their collaboration.

A purely data-driven approach can only go so far in achieving the best outcomes. Calvino points out: 'It's very easy to become quite siloed in *just* trying to analyse the data. Without someone with a creative mind asking, "What does this actually mean? How do we interpret this for something new?" you miss the chance to drive something different.' For her, creativity is crucial in unlocking new possibilities, as teams need someone to ask things like, 'What does that mean?' It's through this mingling of strengths that ideas can flourish beyond what data alone can give.

Don't stay in your lane

Building a successful team also means prioritizing individuals who are proactive, entrepreneurial and bring an authentic sense of responsibility to their work. For Calvino, this mindset goes beyond completing tasks and involves a personal commitment: 'If this was my money, would I actually think this is the right thing for us to be doing? How would I hustle to make sure that this next set of creative or these next set of ads do better?' She highlights the significance of this thinking in smaller teams. Calvino's experience has shown that simply following instructions isn't going to cut it; team members need to think critically and own their roles with a level of accountability. That's what will push the team forward.

Interpersonal skills are equally vital. Successful individuals can navigate the interplay between data and creativity: 'You could be excellent at data analysis, but if you can't talk to the creative team, you're screwed.' Empathy and open communication bridge the natural differences within a team; it's important to help analytical and creative thinkers understand each other's processes and outcomes. Calvino believes that having this understanding is crucial for producing work that is both data-informed and creatively compelling. Team members who 'put their head down and stay in their own lane' miss out on valuable insights from their peers which could enhance the final product.

Currently, Calvino is excited about the unique opportunity to build her team from the ground up – a rare luxury in her career. Unlike previous roles where a predecessor has handed over notes that must be meticulously followed by an incoming employee, she now has the headspace and the time to tailor roles: 'What do we need from this role? How does this role comple-ment someone that we've another? And how does this role then complement someone that we've got in this one?' For Calvino, this 'empty chair' approach, as she calls it, is a strategic way to find roles that not only fill a need but also enhance the team's overall balance and effectiveness.

Calvino values kindness as a foundational quality in any team member, believing it fosters trust, goodwill and cooperation: 'I can't think of a time where someone being nice hasn't worked in their favour. Even if you don't have a clue what you're talking about people will go far to help you because you've been nice and they want to see how you can work together.' She points out that in contrast, poor attitude can have damaging effects: 'If you're not a nice person to work with, why would anyone go above and beyond for you?' To Calvino, being nice is a simple yet powerful 'cheat sheet' for building relationships and nurturing team loyalty. This insight, which has grown stronger with experience, reinforces her conviction that success is often grounded in being a good person, a lesson she finds herself emphasizing more as she continues to lead and grow her team.

Failure vs feedback

Eskridge helped me understand that having a vision for data in the organiza-tion and having a plan for how data is implemented is one thing, but if you don't have the right environment for it to influence creativity then it's not going to fly. Or as former International Development Director at PHD Data Rupert Slade puts it, 'Create an environment that is always questioning – data is information. Questions create insights.'

Calvino's take is that we need to create environments that champion data-led creativity:

> Show teams that although we value data-led creativity, we also need to harness the intuition that enables a safe space for things to fail. As easy as it sounds, saying, 'It's okay for things to fail' goes a long way. As long as we can react quickly, pivot and understand why things didn't perform, then we're still getting something out of it.

Data's role in the organization shouldn't be a straitjacket that squeezes the fun and the experimentation out of a team – it's the opposite. Data should be an enabler of creativity. Calvino stresses the importance of a transparent and encouraging environment:

> If you create an environment where you're just laser-focused on getting things right and things performing well, then there's no space for creativity because things have to fail in some way or another for you to lead on to the next thing. Make sure that you're leading by example and creating a safe space.

I was an Innovation Director at an agency for many years where I learned a harsh truth: in order for one innovation to succeed, many have to fail. There's no roadmap for innovation projects; if there was a process to follow it wouldn't be an innovation. You need teams that are allowed to get it wrong and to ensure that your team is stronger because of the knowledge that the experiment fostered. 'Failing fast' or 'breaking things' isn't the right mindset but 'learning fast through experimentation' is better.

The senior marketers I interviewed for this book had a keen sense for balancing the data with discourse. When speaking to Jim Mollica, President of Luxury Consumer Audio & Chief Marketing Officer at Bose, he affirms the necessity of a safe space for debate as a lot comes from people agreeing and disagreeing: 'You have to make it safe for people to disagree; sometimes it comes from a heartfelt feeling, intuition or instinct that they have. How do we build on those ideas before we shoot them down?'

Data isn't the police force for your marketing but a sidekick for your team's creativity. The way to deliver data and creativity successfully together is by creating the culture that you want. Your data is in the service of your creativity, not the other way around.

Headcount is reducing

We've heard from marketing industry leaders about the role of data in a brand's creative output and the kind of environment that is needed, but what kind of people do you need? There are fewer roles available and an increasing queue of people who are competing for these roles. Head of Martech and AI for Kraft Heinz International, Matt Cosad, highlights this: 'Differentiation in your professional life comes down to fresh technical skills. It's so easy to get complacent in a role and just keep coasting, but from a career perspective pressure is unfortunately only going to increase over the coming years.'

We discussed earlier that the rapid rate of change in the industry is a constant and not a new observation. Cosad's point is that we should be learning new skills and that marketers need to be hiring folk who bring 'new' to the table before they are asked:

> Companies are starting to consolidate producing fewer entities with lower headcount who are able to deliver a similar amount of output as a higher workforce would have in the past. Be competitive, make sure that you're employable by learning new skills and staying at the cutting edge. Doing this stuff in your personal life is a demonstration of passion for it. If you really care about it then you're not stopping when you leave your desk at the office, right?

Cosad concedes, 'In a lot of our creative teams, their passion for creative is funded by working here and they work on other creative projects elsewhere. Having that kind of attitude is hugely important in our teams and for careers in general.'

I've recorded over 250 episodes of the Shiny New Object podcast, which is a show about the future of data-driven marketing. The most lasting impressions from guests come from the people who do exactly what Cosad talks about, people who take their day job skills and put them to use in the evenings and weekends. These types of people can't stop themselves from setting up direct-to-consumer businesses, learning how to build websites, write copy, make and run their own paid media ads. There's a huge list of complementary skills that straddle data and creativity in running a side hustle of this shape. Marketers who are hiring should be looking out for these people. It's these marketers with curiosity and tenacity who will know first-hand how to make creativity and data work wonders.

Why you need humans

You may be thinking that you're going to use AI to cut costs, save time and produce the same amount of work as humans. You may think that the evolution of AI heralds the extinction of human marketers. But I didn't come across a lot of evidence to support this. According to Eskridge, 'You're still gonna need the marketer, I don't think there's a world where that's possible. AI is garbage in garbage out. If you feed it garbage then that's the output you get. You need humans to make sure your output isn't garbage.'

AI isn't *actually* intelligent, it doesn't think. It doesn't do the hard work of observing, empathizing and coming up with ideas that will create the emotion we want. It is great at recreating a sub-standard version of the past that isn't going to surprise your audience or make them feel the love for your brand – you're going to need the right *team* to do that.

Founder of Kepios Simon Kemp and I discussed that the right team for data and creativity is made up of anthropological types, who are people focused rather than tech obsessed. Kemp's view is that if you start with tech, you're going to buy tools that will shape what you do. He sees clients' marketing teams take on a 'project manager' mindset and a tendency to get too much into the weeds. Kemp has seen the fluffy uncertain area of creativity being walked away from in preference for pure data.

Mixing skillsets

Getting the right blend of human-obsessed humans in your team is hard enough, but then getting them to work together well is a whole other thing. Job titles are critically important to most people. They are notches on the bedpost to show we are climbing upwards and at what speed. But this can create separation between people who need to work together and in the worst case it can lead to misunderstanding and animosity. These titles are great for the individual but often less so for the team. As Ceci Dones puts it, 'Why do we have to create labels that keep us afraid of each other or separate from each other or not connected to each other?'

Data and creativity are two different beasts and historically have attracted different people to those roles – fusion is what we're after. As Meredith Herman puts it, 'Diverse minds are more powerful when they are brought together... the best work is that cross-functional teaming where people see things differently.'

Jagdish Sheth sees this as a 'false dichotomy between creative people and data people. There is no such thing as a left brain and right brain; more brains are needed… data experts on my campus have no idea about creativity, we are kept to silos.'

Collaboration is key

Calvino admits that at Brompton Bikes they haven't nailed it yet, but they're focused on having a collaborative process with the creative and performance teams. The way Calvino delivers that is by having the creative and brand team members in performance meetings. This may not be possible in every business but it is crucial for branding teams to have an awareness of campaign performance so that they are able to understand what is actually driving sales.

Jess Burley says:

> Put the data analyst next to the creative, the creative next to the media person, and so on and so forth. By doing this you get those groups of people to respect that an idea can come from anywhere. Collaboration will give you better work. Squashing everybody together encourages curiosity.

A challenge marketers face with making data and creativity work is bridging the gap between data people, marketing people and creative people. This means understanding the business problem, getting the right data and inspiring the creative teams who will come up with the ideas. The challenge is that these teams often speak different languages as well as having different objectives.

I heard once that 'the soft stuff is the hard stuff' – in other words, getting the right people working the right way is what will make the most impact. It's better to have the right people with the wrong tools than to have the wrong people using all the latest tech.

It's their career vs the goal of the brand

It's time for some harsh truths about employees. The reality of any workplace is that people are naturally in the habit of watching their own backs and being more worried about not getting fired than actually pushing the business forward. It's a culture of self-preservation, where short-term career moves outweigh what's best for the product or the company. If your team is more focused on climbing the ladder than on driving real results, you end up with political games and risk-averse behaviour. Editorial Director at Contagious, Alex Jenkins, confirms this simple truth: 'If it's good for the product, but bad for my career, I won't do it. If it's bad for the product, and bad for my career, I don't do it. But, if it's bad for the product and good for my career, I do it.' Leaders are challenged to create an environment where people feel safe enough to take risks and make decisions that might not immediately boost their career, but will ultimately benefit the business. If your team is only motivated by self-preservation, you'll never get the best work out of them.

Multidisciplinary

The cost of building new advertising technology products is getting lower. This will increase competition for marketers' attention and the demand for multidisciplinary talent. As Anastasia Leng observes, the chaotic nature of innovation in the marketing industry calls for 'the rebirth of the renaissance person'. There is a need for marketing pros to be more versatile than ever before. The spiralling complexity of data-driven marketing means that no single skill set will cut it. To navigate this environment, teams *must* blend different disciplines.

Byrne touches on this idea when he discusses the rare quality of 'ambi-dextrous brains', those who can balance both right- and left-brain thinking. The ability to logically read and analyse data while having critical, contextual thinking to give data meaning is becoming increasingly valuable. This skill is rare but necessary as the line between creativity and logic continues to blur. Insight without creativity lacks the emotional connection needed to drive action, and creativity without data can miss the mark entirely.

Despite this, there is often a divide between data-driven and creative professionals. 'Creative people are more mouldable, data people are not,' Sheth says, illustrating the challenge of getting data-centric workers to embrace creativity. Yet, the ability to integrate both is critical in today's market. As Sheth notes, creative minds can more easily be taught to use data, suggesting that the path forward may involve nurturing more flexible thinking in data professionals while continuing to encourage creatives to ground their ideas in actionable insights.

Creative people are not data people

No matter who you are, if you are connecting any kind of data, then you're being creative. Data and creativity can be seen as two separate disciplines – and that's wrong!

When looking to hire creatives, Jon Williams knows exactly what he's looking for: 'Big minds, but big hearts as well.' When it comes to creatives it's key that they are receptive to feedback. Williams looks to onboard those who can produce 'beautiful' work but are open to hearing feedback to improve. He believes this comes down to confidence.

Barbara Galiza's view is that 'a data mindset is absolutely necessary'. Her advice on interviewing someone for a data role is to ask them any question about your company's performance marketing data and 'if they say they need to look at data' they don't know how to deal with data. Galiza's view is that if they express the need to see your data first, then 'they have no idea... when someone (good) looks at data, they already know what the data will be.'

Galiza says that if you ask an interviewee about how to increase the conversion of people from your website's landing page to opening an account, then they should say something like, 'I expect the conversion rates to be between X and Y and then I expect the number of people that drop off to be Z. So therefore, if I want to lift the conversion rate I will try to separate the A, B, C variables.' From a marketing perspective, Galiza's view is that most companies are pretty similar, so a good hire should be able to guesstimate what the data is and create a hypothesis based on this.

Galiza's advice to make creativity and data work together is to employ people who have a divergent *mindset* and a data *skill set*.

Bonuses

This next point is so obvious it's almost not worth mentioning, but working culture often responds to rewards and punishments in one way or another. Jenkins points out that rewards encourage strong performance, in the same way 'holding them over the coals' discourages poor performance. This basic principle can be applied in encouraging the right balance of data and creativity: 'You need to balance encouraging people to interrogate the data while equally rewarding them for making creative leaps from it.' If people are only rewarded for one, you're unlikely to get the other.

This balance is often reinforced through formal structures that balance creativity and data. Creative teams need incentives tied to performance metrics that reflect both the volume and impact of creative output. By doing this, teams know what's expected of them in terms of output and how their work performs.

By integrating these reward systems, enlightened marketers can ensure that both data-driven insights and creative leaps are acknowledged and incentivized. In the end, the right balance of rewards for both data analysis and creative thinking fosters a working culture that values multidisciplinary approaches, driving better outcomes.

Celebrating wins

Once you've incentivized the team financially, then it's a hearts and minds job. Publicly fostering a culture that values data-driven creativity is the way to go. Gaunt points out that it is important to champion the creative use of data: 'The creative use of data needs to be celebrated. There may only be one or two things a year that really help brand growth, but when that happens it needs to be celebrated and shown to the rest of the organization as an example of what you're looking for.' Gaunt's insight underlines the importance of not just using data but making innovative uses of it visible and valued across the company. If we're going to get our teams to put data at the centre of our creativity then there's got to be a culture to support your vision where data-fuelled creativity is shared freely. If you get this right you'll be reinforcing the potential of data-driven creativity to make better work.

Overlapping skills

Wherever you have money, technology and people you will find challenges and marketing is no different. Your teams will need new skills and the ability to have knowledge that connects them to others. The marketing space is changing and the new complexities have given rise to a need for both experts in specialized areas and generalists who need to be able to make sense to each other.

Marketing teams need depth and a balance of skills. The traditional 'T-shaped' profile – a deep expertise in one area complemented by a broad understanding of others – has transformed into what Lex Bradshaw-Zanger calls an 'M-shaped' profile. Marketers today often need 'two or three deep vertical spaces', with hands-on experience in areas like data, trend spotting or content creation. This creates a 'honeycomb network' of specialists, each with unique strengths that overlap and encourage collaborative innovation.

Managing 'M' people requires broad adaptable skill sets from managers that navigate both tech and creativity. Bradshaw-Zanger's career path exemplifies this; he did all sorts from working late nights revising databases to trying his hand at HTML to shaping big ideas with creative directors. His background shows the value of exposing people to various disciplines early in their careers, which fosters well-rounded professionals who can think across fields. This broad exposure aligns with successful careers across all fields. Take for example, the contrasting hyper-specialized path of Tiger Woods, who focused solely on golf, with that of Roger Federer, who dabbled in multiple sports before settling on tennis. This approach creates what David Epstein describes as a 'range' – a toolkit of experiences that allows individuals to view challenges from multiple perspectives and solve problems creatively.[2]

There's a common saying, 'Jack of all trades, master of none', but to Bradshaw-Zanger, this is wrong. He prefers 'Jack of all trades, master of none, can oftentimes be better than a master of one.' He loves a generalist who can bridge the murky world of creativity and the clinical realm of data to connect the dots in ways a pure specialist might struggle with. When people have a variety of experiences, they avoid the trap of viewing every problem through a single lens. Instead, they bring multiple approaches to the table, opening up new pathways for innovation.

The modern marketer's versatility is noted by expert Rupert Slade's idea of 'hybrid people': creatives who understand data and business, data experts who grasp creativity and individuals who see data insight as a game. These hybrids are what we need, making creativity and data inseparable. The ability to switch between analytical and creative thinking allows teams to sweat the data for meaningful insights while giving you the chance to make ads someone might actually notice.

You need to create a world where team members can move between roles, deepening their expertise while gaining breadth. And somehow you need to create moments and experiences that challenge your team to spend time in unfamiliar areas. This will equip them with skills as varied as the demands of modern marketing. The lines between data, creativity and technology are increasingly blurred and only experience will help your team see clearly.

Essential roles in a team

You're going to need a team of marketing Avengers that can handle the complexities of data and creativity. The shifting sands of digital marketing have brought a demand for specialized roles. With this complexity, organizations require a mix of experts, generalists and hybrids to bridge gaps and create cohesive, data-driven yet creative campaigns.

Essential roles in a team are those of the analyst and data scientist. These professionals, according to Sterne, protect the team from the data. Their job is to interpret, contextualize and help decide what data is genuinely valuable. As Sterne emphasizes, collecting data without a clear purpose can lead to wasted resources: 'Unless you know what you want to collect from the data, you're just throwing money away. What question are you actually trying to answer?'

Analysts can be the gatekeepers of the truth, helping teams avoid data overload and focus on insights that drive useful decisions. This distinction between collecting data and generating actionable insights is critical, as Dones further explains: 'The distinction between research, analytics and insights is that researchers are excellent at asking the questions that are meaningful.' Researchers delve into consumer experiences, while analysts bring a statistical background, then insights experts excel at making sense of unstructured data through storytelling.

However, finding an individual who can excel in research, analytics and insights equally is rare, like finding a unicorn, as Dones points out: 'Do you find a unicorn that can straddle all three roles at equal effectiveness? No, they're rare. Extremely rare.' In lieu of such 'unicorns', marketing teams must structure themselves with complementary roles that work together to turn data into insights and insights into ideas.

Attitudes to look for and avoid when building your team

When it comes to building a team you need both qualitative and quantitative people, people with the right attitude. Co-founder of NP Digital, Neil Patel, believes that you either have a culture of people who want to continually improve or one of people who lack passion for the job. These people bode the risk of exhibiting laziness and complacency.

To avoid this, reinforce qualities such as curiosity and creativity. According to Dones:

> Create a culture of curiosity and creativity that requires people who are willing to reinforce values, attitudes, beliefs and norms through repeated rituals. Intuition and data are part of the same toolkit for creativity. It is up to the leader and the surrounding organization to create the psychological safety to utilize all of the tools in the toolkit.

Look for the passionately curious

In the current marketing landscape it is important to be bold. Becky McOwen-Banks highlights the need for 'creator fearlessness' and a 'lack of ego in order to be proved wrong'.

Her team can 'click in to see what insight they were built off – how much spend had been behind them and which cohort they were aimed at'. McOwen-Banks looks for individuals 'passionately curious about things who want to learn', whether they're 'creative thinkers, number people who love the data, or strategists who dig into why people are doing things'. This curiosity and lack of ego help the team stay open minded and adaptable.

McOwen-Banks' advice is to bridge traditional creative lateral thinking with fearlessness. Fearlessness is the ability to just say, 'Well, let's just give it a go'. She notes that she has seen a pattern of this attitude in creators and influencers, who she points out are in touch with their data because they're completely connected to the response. When her team hit a creative rut, she broke them out of their comfort zone, asking them to respond to a brief through Instagram Reels. Setting up fake accounts, she gave her team 36 hours to deliver, pushing them to 'break your brain out of how it is used to thinking', challenging them to embrace the creator mindset of simultaneous conception and execution. This experiment led to AR creative ideas for the Rugby World Cup, embodying her vision of blending the fearlessness of creators with cerebral, lateral thinking to forge a modern approach to marketing.

Do you have deep generalists on your team?

A hunger for continuous learning, as Burley explains, is essential: 'A quality that we look for in the people that we recruit is an appetite for learning; if something comes over your desk that you haven't seen before, you should be thinking "that's interesting!"'

Sheth's concept of the 'deep generalist' adds to this notion, advocating for individuals who, through broad and diverse knowledge, are capable of seeing connections across fields. Sheth encourages the reading of varied sources such as magazines and online journals as they are essential for building a mind that can spot patterns and insights: 'That's the only way to become a deep generalist; you see the connections, you get an "aha" moment.' Such breadth of knowledge fuels innovative thinking and provides a 'toolkit' for approaching problems from different perspectives.

Everybody fails or everybody succeeds

Let's now assume you've got a team of integrated, communicating people with broad and deep experience – the challenge is far from over. Hakan Yurdakul told me:

> The main issue with being part of a big corporation is complex decision-making hierarchies and processes where everybody needs to align. It's not a great thing, because alignment often leads to one of two outcomes: everybody fails or everybody succeeds. This is combined with the fact that everybody's managing their careers in the end, not the business. It becomes a big problem.

In summary, the modern marketing team is a mosaic of skills, mindsets and approaches. By integrating data-savvy individuals who protect and interpret the data, creative thinkers who dare to differentiate and lifelong learners with an appetite for knowledge, organizations can position themselves to navigate the complexities of today's marketing data snake pit. The challenges are substantial, but for those who can build bridges across creative and analytical divides, there will always be a role.

Hiring a team with the right mix of expertise, curiosity and flexibility lays the groundwork for success in an industry with an unpredictable future. The marketing industry requires fearless creators, analytical minds and those who can do a bit of both.

Adaptation is the equivalent to standing still; only aggressive experimentation will get you ahead. And do you know what? Have some fun with it! We've all got to work and all too often we forget the fact that we can enjoy it!

To finish this chapter I'll let Angela Culver have the last word. She draws a powerful analogy to a relay race:

> None of us win until the last person passes the finish line. So, I could be the one that starts off the race, and I pass the baton to the next guy, but if he stumbles and doesn't make it to the third guy, none of us win. Ensure that everyone succeeds. At the end of the day, we're accountable for helping the business grow, and collaboration is the best way to do it.

KEY TAKEAWAYS

- Hire people who naturally blend creative thinking and data skills – those unicorns do exist.
- Create a culture where your team can experiment and fail without fear.
- Communicate the role you want data to play so everyone's on the same page.

Notes

1   Navarro, H (nd) The truth of the monkey ladder experiment, Factschology, factschology.com/factschology-articles-podcast/monkey-ladder-experiment-truth (archived at https://perma.cc/6XUN-AD9S)

2   Epstein, D (2019) *Range: Why generalists triumph in a specialized world*, New York: Riverhead Books

08

Turning data into inspiration

Audience research sounds easy enough – just figure out what people want, right? But people are weird, irrational and rarely say what they actually think. Here's how top marketers figure out what makes people tick and click.

'It's very hard to get to know a consumer on a PowerPoint presentation,' says Lex Bradshaw-Zanger, and this is echoed by Becky McOwen-Banks, who says, 'I think decks are just a place to hide'. It's annoying that the cold, silent digital data that is so abundant and at our fingertips is really just the shadows of people and that unearthing truth from quantitative research is time consuming, expensive and problematic.

But that is the nature of research, and in this chapter we will dig into how to make these two disciplines work together.

The challenge we all have when researching audiences is the fact that people are irrational. This isn't new news but, as Simon Kemp sees it, 'There's some weird notion in an awful lot of the marketing industry that there is this holy grail of this data point that we will find that will somehow unlock everything, and we'll be able to predict it with it.' Unfortunately for us, Kemp sees 'zero evidence that that will ever be the case'. His view is that as soon as you start to understand people, they change their behaviour anyway.

Tom Goodwin's take on this is a little more rosy, saying, 'It's our job to respect people and to understand their motivations and I think the most amazing thing about our job is that we're really lucky. It's our job to try and understand people and people are amazing. They're weird. They're irrational.'

So, let's see how that might be done.

The harsh truth is that it's hard work

Research is and will continue to be both a refined art and a messy science that balances data-driven insights with human curiosity. This chapter explores how you're going to have to bridge the gap between quantitative metrics and qualitative nudges. To get to the truth you're going to be a traditionalist and a modernist in an uncomfortable marriage, using a range of research methods to connect with consumers.

Conducting usable research is dependent on a combination of listening intently to the actual voice of the consumer and blending both real-world encounters and digital interactions. As Faris Yakob emphasizes, 'The voice of the consumer is not statistical inferences of large datasets; it's what real people are feeling and thinking in the world.' By examining digital and real perspectives, this chapter highlights how industry experts prioritize curiosity, context and a blend of the old and new to uncover actionable insights that you might be able to use to make better ads.

The most consistent theme in my research into data and creativity is – curiosity. If you're not curious about how to make something better you can't be creative and if you're not curious about the people you're talking to you can't be empathetic, and without empathy you're unlikely to make anything creatively effective.

Or, as Rosie Yakob puts it, you 'either are inherently curious or you are not... I don't know how to teach curiosity.' I guess that if you're this far into this book then you must be at least a little curious, so let's keep going. Aaron Howe has the view that 'The most valuable book in a library is the one you have not read.' He says this because you have to assume that once you know something your competition knows it also.

It all starts with asking the right questions and seeking answers that can help a business grow. We need to start analysing what the correct data sources are and once we have the correct data sources, then we have the foundations of what might be an audience, what might be a behaviour, and then we start thinking about what might be a platform. And it is at that point when the data has done its job and the creativity begins.

Hakan Yurdakul recalls a childhood lesson from his mother, who taught him the importance of phrasing a question thoughtfully. She told him that when a guest visits your home, you shouldn't ask, 'Would you like to drink something?' Instead, you should ask, 'What would you like to drink?' While the two may sound similar, the first can imply that you yourself may not be drinking anything or that offering a drink is optional – 'and that's not how you treat your guests'. Brilliant! You actually need to ask them, 'What would you like to drink?' which is almost not taking a 'no' for an answer. This formative experience taught Yurdakul that 'Asking the right questions is the most important step in creating your data sets.'

Looking at the data in the right way

Meredith Herman adds to this by emphasizing the importance of organized data: 'It all starts with that underlying data and it being organized so that you can make sense of it. What other data do we have? What else do we know? Sometimes at the surface it's not clear.' This underscores the critical need to not only collect data but also to structure and present it in ways that unlock its full potential.

In many organizations, vast amounts of data are collected, with countless tests conducted, yet the insights remain hidden because the data isn't being looked at or acted upon. Sam Gaunt told me that he has observed many instances where huge amounts of data have been collected and that tests are being done and 'potential insights are lying dormant because the data is not being looked at. And no one's kind of working with it.' There are several reasons for this: some people may not see it as their role to interrogate the data, there may be no clear objectives driving the questions that need to be asked, or the data may not be visualized in a user-friendly manner, making interpretation challenging. As Gaunt highlights, 'That visualization bit is really critical.'

Two senses are not enough

Researching an audience that will provide insight that fuels creativity in advertising requires a nuanced approach that goes beyond simple metrics or trends. To understand consumers deeply, it's vital to see data not as a standalone tool but as a means to get into the mindset of those we're trying to reach. As McOwen-Banks puts it, 'I like sorting out messy bits of spaghetti.' McOwen-Banks uses data to decode the mindset of the consumer at specific moments in time, like knowing if they're commuting. If the audience were commuting then this would call for brief and punchy content in contrast to when they're at home in front of the television, where they're more open to longer-form messaging.

To capture real human insights, we must use all our senses, not just rely on visual and auditory inputs. As Jagdish Sheth emphasizes, 'You need to have five sensory inputs into your brain. Just visual and audio is not enough.' Real understanding of our target audiences comes from tapping into the rest of our senses and when possible experiencing the role of the products we wish to sell first-hand.

Tiffany Rolfe, a creative from Oklahoma now living in New York, speaks to this idea, reflecting on how her own 'data from growing up in Oklahoma is very different than [her] data from New York'. She notes that using data meaningfully requires access to a wealth of experiences, as well as an understanding of different communities, places and needs. When used wisely, data becomes more than just numbers but a pathway to insights that spark ideas that cut through the noise.

This human-centred approach means sniffing out data that reflects consumers' real lives. 'The best strategy,' Rolfe explains, 'is validated by real human, lived experiences.' She cautions against relying solely on generalized data sets. While statistics can guide direction, the real power of data lies in 'unpacking the real story behind it'. It's in these stories that the genuine emotional connections lie, offering a route to creative solutions that resonate with audiences.

In order to dig into qualitative data that is 'the real human stories and insights' requires a proactive approach, according to Rolfe. Finding these stories often involves stepping beyond the numbers, questioning the data and conducting your own research. 'You can't blindly follow the numbers,' she adds. 'You have to dig in and find the stories that exist behind those.'

Without these human stories, data lacks the depth needed to connect our targets emotionally. Instead of viewing data as a rigid guide, Rolfe suggests it be used as a validation tool. Data can help inform decisions about creative direction but can't, on its own, create work that surprises. As Rolfe concludes, 'It just helps validate... but it won't help you actually get to the work that connects with people in a human way.'

There's just so much data to look at

If someone moans about how much data there is in advertising, throw a book at them. Of course there is! It's not an insight to say this, it's obvious. The reason there is so much data is that there are so many people; getting annoyed about the amount of data we have to look at is like moaning about the number of people.

Lex Bradshaw-Zanger's take is that 'the competitive advantage will probably be in the datasets'. His brands constantly refresh and update their research across diverse categories like fragrance, makeup, skincare, haircare and hair colour and are always researching to stay relevant. But for Bradshaw-Zanger, gathering data in itself is the means and not the end. The real challenge is understanding which data points carry weight and which are just noise. He remarks, 'You always have more data than you need, but only when you have everything do you see what the weak signals are and what the strong signals are.'

When data is collected at a global scale, as Sheth describes, it often consists of millions of observations that can be broken down by countries, cultures, demographics and lifestyles, giving insights not only for creative but also for media strategies. Yet, as Faris Yakob points out, 'Big data is data that is so large you can't work it out yourself; you need a machine to look at it.' Without the right tools or objectives, vast amounts of data can quickly become unmanageable.

This sheer volume also brings risks of superficiality. Sinem Kaynak observed early in her career that brands' ambitious data collection efforts often lacked depth. While companies eagerly gathered first-party data, much of it consisted of basic contact details like names, emails, locations, which provided little valuable insight. For Kaynak, meaningful data collection requires a reciprocal value exchange. Consumers should feel motivated to share richer information about their experiences and opinions, which can only happen if they get value in return. Otherwise, she argues, collecting data becomes a wasted effort.

However, without clear objectives or effective methods of visualization, as Gaunt notes, vast datasets often lie dormant, their potential unrealized. He's observed that, across many organizations, data is gathered, stored, and even analysed superficially, with little attention to extracting actionable insights. 'Particularly at junior levels,' Gaunt adds, 'people just ended up collecting data, and then regurgitating that data and putting it in front of people.' The outcome? Long, yawn-inducing presentations that end up losing their audience due to information overload, lacking the depth that would actually add value.

Bradshaw-Zanger emphasizes that true creative insights emerge when data is paired with the right methodologies. The best researchers, he explains, can blend multiple methods to develop a rounded understanding, allowing them to find new truths before using other data sources to verify that data.

Finally, brands must assess the extent of data they truly need. As Kaynak points out, the answer depends on brand type: 'Are you the kind of high-consideration brand that needs a lot of data? Or just go for mass reach?' This point carries so much weight for me. If you are delivering a mass-reach, one-size-fits-all message then how much granularity of data is needed? If your product has a clear point of difference and you know the emotional value it delivers to the audience then it may be a poor use of resources to look deeper.

This is different if you have a mid- to high-level consideration product where many factors come into play during the buying decision – then you're going to need to dig a lot deeper. Effective use of data, then, requires more than just collection; it involves purpose, skill and interpretation, transforming raw information into insights that inspire something that someone, somewhere might pay attention to.

Advertisers should be like detectives

Collecting the right amount of data and not getting swamped by the noise of 100 dashboards is a task in its own right. Once you have the right data, you need to look at it in the right way. This process resembles detective work, as Rory Sutherland describes, which operates in two distinct phases: investigative and evidential. He compares it to police work, where detectives first gather leads and observations that may or may not prove valuable. 'In police detective work,' he explains, 'there are kind of two phases. There's what you might call the first phase, which is exploratory, it's investigative. And the second phase, which is evidential.' This distinction reveals an important point: while data and evidence matter, not every piece of information has immediate evidential value.

In the marketing world, Sutherland suggests, the exploratory phase involves asking unconventional questions and seeking patterns or anomalies that may not immediately seem valuable. 'If we don't allow those kinds of… exploratory procedures in problem solving, then we're only exploring a very limited part of the possible solution space,' he adds. This view points to the importance of flexibility in data interpretation, which is a mindset that resists the urge to dismiss information simply because it doesn't fit traditional evidential criteria.

This idea of discovery, or 'seeing something new in the data', contrasts with more rigid interpretations that only focus on immediate evidential data.

Sutherland provides an example with coffee shops and their closing times: 'The standard interpretation would be that demand for coffee falls off as we pass 3:30,' he notes. 'And that is indeed a perfectly valid theory.' Sutherland suggests an alternative explanation, that customers might avoid a coffee shop close to closing time because of subtle behaviours like the staff putting chairs upside down on tables or cleaning espresso machines. These are gentle signals to customers that they are unwelcome. This leads to what he calls 'getting the mop out', where employees signal an early close to avoid serving last-minute customers. The data may show reduced sales late in the day, but Sutherland points out that these are 'not the reason for your closing at four o'clock. It's actually a product of your closing at four o'clock.' This concept of reversed causality where we mistake A for causing B when actually B caused A challenges researchers to consider not only what the data shows but also why certain patterns exist, requiring a deeper look into behaviours and perceptions rather than surface-level numbers alone.

Editorial Director at Contagious, Alex Jenkins, illustrates how this detective-like mindset can lead to unexpected discoveries. He recounts stories where anomalies in data have led to groundbreaking products: 'Pfizer was trying to create a drug to treat heart conditions,' he explains, and stumbled upon what would later become Viagra after observing an unexpected side-effect. The same insight applies to the Post-it Note, where a scientist seeking a strong adhesive accidentally created one that was weak but reusable.[1] 'So, same data, different way of looking at it,' Jenkins notes. 'Instead of throwing away Viagra and Post-it Notes because they didn't work as intended, they saw potential in these unexpected outcomes.' In research, this mindset of asking 'So what?' allows brands to turn anomalies into opportunities, turning what might have been failures into new and profitable products.

Reach out and touch someone

The art of 'seeing something new' in data also extends to understanding human connections and emotions, which raw data alone cannot capture. Sheth shares an example from a segmentation study for AT&T, in which the data revealed that family relationships were a driver of long-distance calls. Originally, without this data the agency created a sentimental ad that missed the mark. 'So we changed around,' Seth says, 'and we said "reach out and touch someone", just to call.' This simple tagline, rooted in data yet emotionally resonant, brought a depth that data points alone couldn't deliver. 'All came from data, operational data,' Sheth reflects, showing how creative interpretations of data can connect with audiences on a personal level, blending human insight with statistical analysis.

For those working with massive datasets, maintaining this curiosity-driven approach is challenging but essential. Gaunt emphasizes the role of effective visualization, where data needs to be presented in a way that emphasizes its meaning rather than its volume. He critiques common practices that result in 'overly detailed presentations where, by the end of an hour, no one in that room is paying any more attention'. This often happens, he suggests, when analysts simply 'regurgitate data' without adding value through interpretation or visualization. Researchers must consider data points as scenes in a story and not a dispassionate list of things that happened. Gaunt's view is that properly visualized data helps reveal hidden patterns and insights, making it accessible to those without technical chops.

Yurdakul offers insight into the limitations of traditional advertising testing. Most tests focus on benchmarks that attempt to capture reactions from a broad audience, producing 'super standard ads that do not move the needle much'. He explains that in a crowded market, ads that adhere to these standards often fail to stand out. Instead, Yurdakul suggests targeting niche audiences with distinctive ads that break traditional norms: 'Finding those creatives that are creating really huge buzz by finding these differentiating distinctive niches is the way to go.' In his view, relying too heavily on norms stifles creativity, while leaning into data to identify polarizing or unconventional choices can lead to breakthrough moments. Rolfe reinforces the importance of digging into data for unique insights that align with human behaviours and stories. She argues that 'as a curious, creative person, you're always looking for something that might be undiscovered'.

The act of seeing something new in the data demands an investigative mindset, the ability to look beyond immediate interpretations and a hunger to understand the human. For Sutherland, this requires that researchers move beyond mere evidential data to maximize 'exposure to upside optionality'. By noticing anomalies, questioning causality and getting under the skin of the audiences we're after we can unlock new sources of inspiration.

Hocus focus

In my research for this book, one of the questions I was particularly interested in was how brands can bridge the gap between quantitative cold data and qualitative claimed data. When someone clicks on an ad, there's very little data on why that happened; conversely, when consumers share their feelings about a brand there's a gap between what they say and reality.

Neil Patel's approach is to sync the quantitative data that he gets from platforms like Facebook with the qualitative data he gets from speaking to the target audience. He will actively quiz his audiences about ads that he has run and 'ask their opinions and try to find out more'. Patel will ask, 'What do you like to see in an ideal product? What would you like to see in ads? You know, what resonates with you, why did you buy this product? Or why would you buy this product? What do you like about the competition versus this company?' The process is to get insights and then share creatives so that 'we're getting insights on both ends'. His belief is that it's the words that go with the ones and zeros that give more insights on 'how to tweak the winning variations and make it even better'.

Patel's solution is combining quant and qual data, 'The ones and zeros tell you what people are actually doing, not what they're saying. You talk to people, you get the real reason behind the action.' He concedes that 'It doesn't always align up as one would think', but 'it just makes your campaigns more likely to be successful in the future.'

This is a compelling and clear distinction – what are people saying versus doing? It's exciting that there is data on both but what we will never get is the ability to get data on what people are thinking. We can observe the brain in action and observe the outputs of the brains in the form of actions and words – but we can't know what our customers are actually thinking. So we have to make do with getting data on what consumers did and what they said.

Trust

Kaynak is seeing a shift in how we gather insights about what consumers really want. She points out that traditional methods like focus groups are falling out of favour. Their limitations, like not reaching enough people and potential biases, make them less reliable. She's excited about the possibilities AI brings to the table, especially in analysing vast amounts of data for fresh insights. For Kaynak, real-time data from online conversations, trending topics and conversation sentiment are important. She trusts AI to sift through these conversations accurately, merging the depth of qualitative insights with the precision of quantitative data.

In recent times the value of qualitative research has often been overshadowed by a focus on quantitative data. As Peter Field points out, 'We haven't talked much in this conversation about the value of qualitative research, and it's been, I think, much overlooked and dismissed in the last decade or so in favour of big-scale kind of cold data.' It's Field's view that this shift towards a numbers-only approach has sometimes led to neglecting the rich, nuanced insights that qualitative methods can provide.

Everybody lies

The limitations of relying solely on quantitative methods are evident. Jim Sterne bluntly states, 'You don't *just* do surveys, because everybody lies.'

Surveys and statistical analyses can miss the subtleties of human behaviour and emotions. But Bradshaw-Zanger shares a personal affinity for more intimate research settings: 'I love sitting behind the mirror in qualitative focus groups.' These environments allow researchers to observe and understand participants' underlying motivations in a way that numbers alone cannot capture.

Yurdakul strongly believes that qualitative methods are far superior in capturing human opinions and behaviours. He argues that traditional survey-based research, which relies heavily on closed-ended questions, fails to reflect how people naturally think and interact. 'Do you ask your friends, family, or loved ones, "How much do you love me on a scale of one to ten?" Hopefully not,' he points out. To Yurdakul, this kind of questioning is 'not the natural way of interacting with real human beings.' He believes that true understanding comes from conversations, not from filling out forms. Yet, he observes that the industry still defaults to these rigid, uninspired methods. Questions like 'On a scale of one to ten, how much do you like this ad?' or 'How likely are you to buy this product?' dominate research, reducing human emotions to data points. While Yurdakul acknowledges that closed-ended questions still have a place, he insists they should emerge naturally within a conversation rather than defining the entire engagement. His mission is to change, he explains, 'that closed-ended questions are not natural – they're artificial, a borderline fake setup that fails to truly explore consumer minds.'

For Yurdakul the output of these bland and generic questions is usually an 'ideal version of the surveyor; they tend to tell you either only the obvious or the best version of an answer'. His solution is using an AI-powered qualitative research tool to conduct user interviews. In Yurdakul's experience of building his company, when AIs conduct the research there are two things that are different compared to human-to-human conversation. First, users don't feel as intimidated: 'People feel more secure and anonymous talking to an AI – that's why they open up more.' And second, because it's a conversation AI can actually go deeper into some of those insights: 'Apart from the obvious, so you create a secure, safe environment where you can ask deeper and deeper questions, yet do not intimidate the respondent.'

So there's a chance we'll be telling AIs 'how likely we are to buy this product', but however the questions are delivered by AI or the meat-based alternative – we need to ask the right questions. There's a consensus that a balanced approach between quant and qual is essential. As Tash Beecher emphasizes, 'The important thing is to get both, a mixture of both that doesn't just rely on one or the other.' Combining quantitative data with qualitative insights leads to a more comprehensive understanding of consumers.

Don't let your bias be your baseline

An illustrative example comes from Yurdakul, who recounts a transformative experience during a business trip to Egypt. As the brand manager for an anti-dandruff shampoo called Clear, which doesn't exist in Europe but is popular in Asia and is the biggest competitor of Head & Shoulders, they had a famous athlete as the brand ambassador. 'I have done a couple of consumer visits,' he recalls. 'I visited a different range of consumers, from higher affluence to those not living in great conditions.'

During one visit, while discussing shampoo habits with a father, a seven-year-old boy emerged, bringing used 5 ml sachet packs of the shampoo featuring the athlete's image. 'This was actually my birthday gift,' the boy told him. 'Because I love him. My dad got it for me, and I kept it because I love him.' This encounter was eye-opening. What was merely a promotional item in one context became a cherished possession in another.

'It gave me that perspective of how you need to look at data and how you need to interpret it,' Yurdakul reflects. 'It's so easy to get lost in looking into numbers and just taking data as data, but especially in the context of marketing and advertising and brand development, there's so much under the surface.' This experience reinforced the importance of delving deeper into consumers' lives and interactions with products. 'You need to really go under the surface, look deeper, really understand consumers, their lives, and how you interact with them,' he adds. 'That was the first moment when I kind of fell in love with consumer data and how you need to look into it and interpret it.'

Have an intuition mission

Similarly, Tina Eskridge shared a story about working on a project targeting African American female entrepreneurs. The existing data suggested they had exhausted their total addressable market, but Eskridge's intuition told her otherwise. 'There's probably something else that we're missing,' she thought. She decided to explore other content sources with cultural and contextual relevance beyond the data she had at hand.

Digging deeper, she realized, 'They don't source data the same way as the rest of your small and medium business owners.' This audience wasn't going online; instead, 'They're going to meetups in their communities for entrepreneurs. Then that's where you need to be.' The original data set hadn't revealed this insight; Eskridge had to delve further. She believes that the hard work of going to 'meet them where they are' is the only way to determine how to engage with them effectively.

Tina has observed a rise in cultural and contextual data availability but still values 'the tried and true way of doing focus groups, just on the ground, talking to people the good old-fashioned way.' Her approach involves having a hypothesis when tackling any problem and then diving into the data to see if there's a match to her initial expectations. 'Have a hypothesis going into any problem that we're trying to solve,' she advises, and then explore the data to confirm or adjust that hypothesis.

Cat and mouse pad

The challenges of measuring human emotions and psychology further highlight the limitations of quantitative data. Sterne observes, 'It's trying to measure psychology and humans, so I can measure mouse movements and click-throughs and page views. But measuring an emotional response to a stimulus is something that we don't have our arms wrapped around yet.' While technologies like fMRI machines can provide insights into brain activity in response to emotional stimuli, 'that's so wildly expensive,' he notes.

Given these constraints, he suggests a more practical approach: 'It is easier to brainstorm great ideas with really smart people, and test a bunch of things to see what lands, and then try to learn from the past.' This highlights the value of creativity and human insight over relying solely on data.

The right research is going to take time and effort but there's clear guidance for marketers here. Ask questions of your audience, accept it's not all going to be the truth, then test your hypothesis using quantitative data and see what worked. And then take what worked and ask your audience why they reacted the way they did. The way forward according to these seasoned experts is to dance between confusing qual and cold quant.

Conversations before conversions

For Barbara Galiza, qualitative data is the starting point for performance marketing campaigns: 'You need to have information from the customer, from the audience. That would usually come from qualitative data. I think the most common form of that is user interviews.' This is a highly surprising opinion to me from probably the most experienced performance marketer I spoke to.

'Qualitative is where the first insights will come; creativity is how you execute.' Galiza talks about her work on a dating app for queer women. She conducted interviews with women who would often say that they used the app to 'make friends'. When Galiza used follow-up questions like 'How did you decide which person to start a conversation with?' the respondents would say 'By the way they look' – which is an interesting way to choose a friend on a dating app. This piqued Galiza's interest. She mused on the reality that 'making friends' was how users were communicating the value they got from the app but not *why* they were really using it. They said they were using the app to make friends, but they were actually using it to find partners – but didn't feel comfortable admitting at a time in history when dating apps weren't socially accepted as a norm.

So Galiza's hypothesis was that if she ran 'make some friends' messages in her ads they would perform better and they did, significantly. Her theory was that these ads were being served at a time when women in that market 'were more on the back foot' with dating apps. So softer messaging that focused on community and friendship resonated. She took this insight one step further and helped the organization create new features and an onboarding that focused on events and community-led features. Despite these features not being used a lot, it gave the app something to promote that 'was the most successful messaging for us when it comes to user acquisition.'

If the business had spoken to their users about their favourite features, then the result would have been very different. Despite qualitative research being the primary inspiration Galiza warns that user interviews should be taken with a grain of salt and 'always make sure that you're comparing user interviews with actual data'.

Rolfe's view is that a lot of people have 'access to the same type' of qualitative or quantitative data and that qualitative data is better because this gives the creative mind access to real stories and scenarios, and whoever finds the best insight in those or puts the data together in the most unique way is what 'kind of wins'.

Digital data is abundant but doesn't tell the whole story and in-person interviews are slow, expensive and can't always be trusted. So we're in a tough spot getting these to work together well but each can raise questions that the other can answer. Does an insight from a user interview lead to an effective digital outcome and does a data-driven trend make sense when you are talking to a customer? The truth ebbs and flows between the hard digital records and soft human interactions. Neither is perfect but they have the ability to shine the light on each other to reveal the truth we are all after.

Constantly researching

'What are people talking about on TikTok this month?' asks Bradshaw-Zanger, highlighting the need for a steady flow of insights to be circulated throughout his organization. Staying at the forefront of product development means understanding not just current trends but also how to actively engage with them. 'What are the trends, and how do I lean into them?' Bradshaw-Zanger continues, emphasizing the importance of being proactive. The focus isn't solely on fleeting trends but also on major global movements: 'It's the high-level view of what's going on,' he explains, from shifts in skincare – from cleansing and acne to anti-ageing, serums and daily sun care – to how these trends unfold at different speeds across markets: 'You see things happening at different speeds in different markets. You know, acne is big somewhere else, or serum is super exciting, or what ingredients people are talking about.'

This granular understanding of consumer behaviour is complemented by broader explorations of audience interests. 'Who are those people? What are they interested in? What entertainment are they engaging with? What do they spend the most time researching on the internet? What sources are they looking at? What are their attitudes when it comes to purchase?' says Perla Bloom, illustrating how layered data helps inform effective ideas. 'All of these levels of data will answer that,' Bloom adds, showing how interconnected insights fuel both creativity and strategy.

Our job is qual

In adland our first job is to walk in the shoes of customers and live their behaviours, motivations and experiences. As Goodwin puts it:

> I actually think our entire job is 'qual'. I could go on and on about this for quite a long time. Our job is to understand people. If we were quite sensible 85 per cent of the time, you know, we'd be on a bus going to Swindon. 85 per cent of our time we'd be in Wetherspoons at Reading Station. 85 per cent we'd be in a sort of library that's about to close down in the Outer Hebrides, and we would just be immersing ourselves in what it is to be a human all day long.

This immersion isn't just about gathering data; it's about empathizing and genuinely trying to grasp why people make the decisions they do, especially regarding the products they buy.

Qualitative research allows us to delve into individual experiences, offering insights that numbers alone can't provide. Rolfe mentions, 'I did tend to dig in more to qualitative data, like the real interviews with people. And getting kind of deeper into individual experiences.' By engaging directly with individuals, we uncover the nuances of human behaviour that quantitative data might overlook.

Get out, do the research, meet the people

Ceci Dones appreciates chief marketing officers who prioritize the consumer's voice: 'If I take a consumer-centric point of view, which is where I really love all my CMOs because they're the only voice sometimes in some boardrooms of the consumer.' And we can't be the voice of the customer if we haven't listened to them in the first place.

Qualitative research can help us understand the reality of our products' roles in our targets' lives. It's not without its shortcomings but it has value that purely tech-driven alternatives will miss. Field emphasizes that qualitative research when it's done well 'grounds you'. He suggests that 'going to listen to a bunch of real hard-pushed, hard-stretched consumers in the less advantaged areas of your country, your culture, will teach you a hell of a lot'. He points out that they're not all wearing 'Meta specs and they don't have 15 digital devices in their bedrooms'. His view is that they live in a much tougher real world than the ones 'hotshot marketers' live in. He urges us to 'Get out, do the research, meet the people, talk to the people, and find out what really goes on in their world' by stepping out of our Shoreditch-based, flat white-sipping comfort zone and interacting with those we seek to influence.

E.V.s and E.D.

A practical example of the power of qualitative insights comes from Jess Burley's experience working with Toyota across Europe. At the time, hybrid cars were successful but faced perception issues. 'Hybrid was a very successful format for Toyota, but there was a mystique around the perception of why certain buyers didn't buy a hybrid,' she explains. Diesel buyers, in particular, were resistant due to misunderstandings about the technology and a belief that hybrids weren't for them. 'There was a perception amongst certain cohorts that hybrid was for a particular type of person,' she notes. Some thought hybrids were 'a bit cool' or 'a bit right on', leading them to believe, 'I'm a regular mum or I'm a businessman... that's not for me.'

To address this, they used a recontacting strategy across various consumer groups. 'The commonest thing was when you spoke to the people that had bought hybrid, it was an active choice,' Burley says. They discovered that consumers chose hybrids for multiple reasons – not just for fuel economy or environmental benefits. This insight allowed them to advise Toyota:

> We need to stop talking about the technology. We need to stop talking about the performance of the engine, which was their preferred communication method. And we actually need to talk about why consumers choose hybrid. And by the way, in our communications, we need to show the fact that it's multiple reasons, not just one reason.

The resulting campaign, 'We Choose Hybrid', showcased the diverse reasons people opted for hybrids. This shift led to significant sales increases: 'Sales in that year, which I think was 2016 or 17, were at 8.6 per cent against a market which was down 6.9 per cent.' By understanding consumers on a deeper level, they transformed hybrids into Toyota's best-performing sales asset.

Another compelling story highlighting the importance of deep qualitative research involves a project on erectile dysfunction. Beecher shares, 'I have done a lot of work on erectile dysfunction as a topic – literally got nothing to do with me on all forms. I am not a cis man.' Despite not having a personal connection to the issue, she delved into the data to address a significant problem. The client had a therapy cream for erectile dysfunction that worked effectively, but men weren't using it correctly. 'All of the data suggested that it works really well, but there was a problem in that men weren't using it properly,' Beecher explains.

By drilling down into the data and seeking to understand the real human issues, they realized the need for clearer communication. Collaborating with her art director at the time, Rachel Lamb, they came up with the line 'Tackling E.D. one drop at a time' and designed a logo emphasizing precision with a 'drop' symbol. 'We managed to make the logo so that it was this drop, to represent the accuracy of getting this cream in, because it was a cream that came with a little pipette dropper thing,' Beecher says. This approach addressed the problem by highlighting correct usage, ultimately helping men benefit from an effective treatment. 'Again, it's kind of drilling down into that data to validate that real human issue that people are having,' she reflects.

How tech can help do better qual

Field notes, 'In the last 10 to 15 years the kind of data collected about creativity and creative executions has become much more aligned to genuine neuroscience; it's starting to become very helpful.' Modern testing methods examine the impact of advertising on people's emotional responses. 'They look at how interesting, how stimulating it was on an emotional level, and there are different kinds of emotions,' he explains. These models correlate with effectiveness and when used sensitively 'can actually help us improve creativity and help us make sure that creativity is aligned to effectiveness'.

While focus groups sometimes receive criticism, they remain a valuable tool in understanding consumer perspectives. Jon Williams' focus is to try to make everything 'platformized'. He tries to 'digitize everything that we can'. His focus is to try to make sure that his research methodology is faster so that he 'can research in any market, in any demographic, anywhere in the world, and get a response'. For Williams it's about quickly working out what is not resonating, knowing that 'if you change that, you'll course correct'. Williams is progressive in his use of combining old-school curiosity with newer digital methods. This allows him to reach a broader audience more efficiently while still capturing the depth of human experiences.

Traditional qualitative research is slow, expensive, can't be entirely trusted and is often dependent on a small group of respondents. However, the alternative is to not be curious, not ask questions and ignore the opportunity to listen and learn. If this is your approach then you're left with 1s and 0s which, though abundant, tell their own lies.

Getting useful research, not just noise

Bloom uses data to make sure her teams don't lose sight of the creative solution that will achieve the business objective they are after. 'So we'll always depend on the objectives set out at the beginning.' It's about choosing the right data for the right job. If Bloom is looking to bridge a gap between the business need and the consumer, then that's when culture-level data will come into play. This kind of data will be something that aligns with what they are doing outside of the product. If you're sense-checking the idea for a big campaign, 'You need focus groups and qualitative data,' but 'if you're trying to understand what creative works best on what channel and when, then quantitative data is going to be best for this'.

Bloom likes to go after a broad set of different types of data. She asks, 'Who are those people? What are they interested in? What entertainment are they engaging with? What do they spend the most time researching on the internet? What sources are they looking at? What are their attitudes when it comes to purchase?' Bloom uses all these resources to inspire the idea that's going to do the job and 'these levels of data will answer that'. And it's not plain sailing with qualitative data: 'It doesn't tell the whole story – you might be seeing a correlation versus causation.'

Reporting back the good stuff

My observation in agencies is that the volume of data is often mistaken for value. The crutch of many agency workers (myself included) has been to present complex information at length that makes perfect sense and gives absolute clarity – to the author. I've spent many evenings fine-tuning presentations that hit the nail on the head in the knowledge that when I present these findings the audience will break out into applause. This never happened. The first act of presentation writing is to convince ourselves and the second is to scrap the first and then write it for the audience. Poorly presented data is redundant data. It's our job to get the story and share it in a compelling way.

This highlights a central challenge in research for data-driven marketing that data needs to be contextualized and connected to the real world. Multidisciplinary expert Ceci Dones shared a formative experience with me. Early in her career, Dones observed a focus group testing digital ads that tried to replicate print formats. It was not the numerical data that struck Dones, but the nonverbal reaction of a participant who was a middle-aged lady struggling to read text in a cluttered, tiny ad. Watching her repeatedly adjust her glasses to squint at the screen revealed more about the ad's shortcomings than digital data ever could.

This moment became a powerful learning experience for Dones. Despite initial resistance from the client, this human response became pivotal evidence to advocate for better design solutions: 'That initial experience of watching someone take their glasses on and off to squint... that's when I realized, oh gosh, you need to figure out how to do this bit better,' she reflects. It was a reminder that qualitative insights and human reactions can sometimes illuminate truths that numbers alone cannot.

Once again we see the value of research isn't in the volume of data but in its interpretation, and if it is presented well then it can make us better marketers. Researchers must move beyond data crunching and actively engage with the human behind the numbers.

You won't get a second first impression

Part of my job at Automated Creative is to market our own business to marketers. One of the most directly useful pieces of business-to-business marketing advice I received while researching this book was from Galiza. She sees real value in 'the first contact that you have with someone that's interested in purchasing your product'. She suggests asking them about their pain points before you pitch your service.

The first connection with a potential customer when they are not 'polluted by all your additional messaging already' is the moment to listen and understand them. 'So trying to understand really, what problem are they trying to solve? How are they communicating this problem? How do they think you solve this problem? Why do they think you solve this problem?' This has helped me not take our potential clients' positions for granted.

Galiza's advice is that once you've interviewed your audience while they don't know a great deal about, you to gain insights you then have to test the hypothesis. The test has to be a metric-driven 'true or false' one. So you need to be able to test your hypothesis and be confident that the answer is either yes or no. This is the opposite of trawling through analytics platforms looking for something interesting. Galiza's problem with looking through data is that 'there's so many varietals that you haven't set yourself... that's why I always really prefer to do controlled experiments'.

Listening to your audience

McOwen-Banks' goal as a creative is 'not to get lots of people to feel virtually nothing' but to find a 'rich vein of people who really do feel the passion for a brand' and social comment data gives her that because they've 'invested time and brain space' to write in words an actual response.

McOwen-Banks gives the example of New Balance trainers, who historically portrayed themselves as a brand for elite top sports people. In her view, 'there's a massive gap there' and the brand was not being honest about who its customers were or its role in their lives. The reason for this was that before social data became available, brands could put any ads out into the world that they liked 'because there was never any feedback loop, or we rarely paid attention'. If brands didn't do their research, then what they believed was real, and the reality of how the brand was received, were two different things. McOwen-Banks' view was that there was 'sometimes a massive gap between those two positions'.

McOwen-Banks' creative approach is to be 'a little bit geeky' and wanting to get into where the data comes from, whether it's quant or qual. She sees it as important to 'get out in the world, out in the wild, to actually confirm or deny whether those positions actually correlate or actually really what the reality of the work to be done is'.

Don't be a white coat marketer

Even when the creative territory or insight is the same for all channels for a campaign, data can tell us the different times that brands can deliver different types of storytelling. The story must meet with the scenario, and data is our device to do that. Becky's a big believer that social data has allowed us to 'better understand what interests or passions our audience has far more richly... we're more able to speak to people less as demographics and more through interests'. In her opinion, 'No one wants to be a friend of an insurer on Facebook. They're not my friends... I don't want to follow them.'

This isn't an attack on financial services brands but McOwen-Banks' philosophy is based on using data to keep you honest. 'You need honesty to go in and use data in a really dispassionate way' and show the reality of the situation of the people you are trying to connect with. It's only by using the data to get an honest view that will allow creative ideas to happen that will get the brand where it wants to be. But most agencies and brands aren't looking at the data in this way, in McOwen-Banks' view, 'because we're too brand indoctrinated, and we're viewing it sort of in a white coat environment as opposed to someone who's living and breathing what they believe, every single day'.

Bloom's take is that social listening can help her find the link between what the brand wants to do and what matters to the consumer 'because that's where your audience is, that's where you're going to have a real edge'. Ultimately for Bloom the best use of data and creativity is dependent on the objective as well as understanding the nature of the sources and how trustworthy they are. However, a key belief of Boom's 'is not to be snobby with data'. She is keen to make sure that when we are collecting data on our audiences not to 'ridicule' people's interests. When brands and agencies are writing briefs she's observed people scoffing at reality TV, music choices or hobbies that aren't immediately relevant to the task in hand, 'but the reality is people are spending most of their time talking, engaging with these kinds of things'. Bloom's view is that people do all kinds of 'silly things' when they are relaxing and trying to escape and these can be one of those 'moments that other brands won't have thought of'.

The danger of only using numbers

The overreliance on numbers poses a significant challenge for organizations. The value of qualitative insights comes alive in examples like Heinz, celebrated by Bloom for its genius use of simple but profound data points.

'Heinz could be really predictable and they actually don't have to be as clever as they are,' Bloom notes. Yet they've built a platform around food's social significance. By identifying that 70 per cent of people globally would rather wait for condiments than eat without them, even if it means a cold meal,[2] they claimed a unique moment in the cultural and social dining experience. This insight transformed Heinz into a hero of everyday rituals, celebrated in campaigns that creatively depict the wait for ketchup, even humorously extending to a man's coffin.

This example illustrates the power of asking the right questions and using data as a catalyst for creativity, rather than a constraint. By observing real behaviours, Heinz turned data into emotionally resonant and entertaining storytelling. 'Data should spark brilliance,' Bloom concludes, emphasizing the critical balance of insight and creativity. Heinz's campaigns demonstrate how being curious, asking the right questions and using the right data enables executions that people are talking about long after the ads are shown.

An unusual articulation of this was shared with me by Bradshaw-Zanger. McDonald's picked up the trend of customers enjoying dipping chicken nuggets in their sundaes. And because McDonald's has access to the data on who buys what with what, combined with powerful 'big business insights', this enables them to look at the correlations between products and 'how many orders have gotten nuggets and sundaes together.' McDonald's then developed the product in certain countries where the sundae came with the nuggets already on top.

Yurdakul encourages people to look for 'distinctive niches' like sundaes and nuggets. His view is that advertising creative is currently tested by sending ads to a nationally representative sample of around 200 people. Their reactions are compared against historical benchmarks, which gauges the general population's reaction. Yurdakul has observed that this approach misses the mark in today's fragmented, congested, 'red-ocean market'. His view is that the way to stand out isn't through norms and standards – it's by finding 'diamonds' outside traditional boundaries. He explains that the 'real magic happens' when you step beyond the norms, exploring polarized advertising that creates an emotional reaction. If you aim to win the general population with a heavily averaged approach, you end up with a 'super standard ad' that goes straight into the advertising landfill of ideas people instantly forget about. Instead, the path forward is about finding creatives that can fire emotion, surprise us and be remembered by reaching out from the mainstream and into the dark.

Summary

When it comes to qual, then, encourage your teams to be disciplined in their use of data and make sure they have time and open-mindedness to look at the source, the methodology, the commissioners of the research and the sample size before presenting it as a fact. Equally with quantitative data, make sure your researchers are checking quant with qualitative experience. So if there is a significant or surprising quant insight, ask why this is and if there are any factors that might bias the data. It's not too painful to simply check in with some humans to see if the interesting quant data seems sensible.

KEY TAKEAWAYS

- Not combining quant (what people do) with qual (why they do it) isn't a great idea.
- Don't get tricked by surface-level data – keep asking 'why' and dig deep for the good stuff.
- Insights that will inspire creativity will come from asking questions that your competitors won't think to ask.

Notes

1 Skonord, C (2021) Post-it Notes: An innovative employee idea that was originally a mistake, Ideawake, ideawake.com/post-it-notes-employee-idea-that-was-originally-mistake/
2 Houston, A (2024) Ad of the Day: Heinz knows that hungry customers will wait for its sauce, The Drum, www.thedrum.com/news/2024/01/24/ad-the-day-heinz-knows-hungry-customers-will-wait-its-sauce (archived at https://perma.cc/S33N-CYSS)

09

The metrics that matter and briefs built on insight

'If you're trying to digest all of that data, it's a bit pointless. It's like trying to eat everything in the supermarket when actually all you wanted was an apple.' – Simon Kemp

Getting your hands on a lot of data is easy but measuring the right things is much harder. This chapter is about cutting through the mist of metrics to measure what actually grows your brand.

At Automated Creative we've always been obsessed with the idea of closing the loop between data and creativity. Our experience of agency culture saw that there was a focus on creative ideas being cool or at least Cannes-worthy and not much attention was given to which elements of the creative drove the outcomes that were wanted. So we've made sure that the measurement and metrics of creativity have been our focus for the best part of a decade. That's not to say we've entirely cracked it, no one has, but this chapter gives multiple examples of how to approach the thorny subject of metrics in a world of data and creativity.

The purpose of metrics

Jim Sterne told me, 'You have to have a good product. Yes, you have to have a good price. Yes, you have to promote it in the right places. But if your message is boring and falls flat, nobody cares that you have the best product in the world. Using metrics allows us to determine whether our creative is hitting the mark.'

So this is why we have metrics in place, to see if the work works. But there are many compounding issues such as the fact that 'ad agencies are not the best people to ask if their advertising is effective. It is not in their interest to tell you bad news. I would use a media or tracking company; in a media agency getting data early and acting on it is the trick.' This quote is from the retired media agency CEO Rupert Slade, so he's got no reason to pull punches.

He continues that 'Too much data is just plain information, competitive advertising data is never ending and sometimes so much of an agency's life is about covering themselves and justifying expenditure.' It's forgivable human nature to want to present your work in its best light, but the best light rarely illuminates the truth.

Can you get over the bar?

So let's hope your teams are measuring something and the truth isn't being buried in slides to begin with. First we need to be sure we're asking the right questions of our metrics. As Simon Kemp puts it:

> We've got to stop this obsession with metrics that don't mean anything… I am yet to find a metric that is reported directly by social media platforms that tells me anything useful as a business. These are measures of content performance, they're not measures of business outcome, and the danger is that we become obsessed with those measures of performance… it's very clear that a lot of these metrics are not telling us the answers that we need.

The danger is to measure the easiest thing to hand, not do the hard work to measure the thing that matters.

Kemp uses a sporting analogy:

> I'm doing the high jump, there's only one metric that matters. How fast I run doesn't make any difference, how high I jump is all that matters. But if we're saying, look how fast he's running, and they run faster and faster and faster, it's amazing, doesn't matter. The only thing that matters is the height of that bar and whether you get over it. I think most marketing teams are getting obsessed with metrics that don't matter to the rest of the business because they're not the metrics that matter. And the metrics that matter are not solely in marketing's control.

Kemp is telling us that marketing is its own worst enemy by talking in the language of marketing data alone. Marketing is the servant of the business, not the business itself. Kemp added:

> We've got to stop believing that there is this single answer that is somehow going to work for everybody… because that's not differentiating. If everybody

was doing the same thing, we're all following the same model and approach, everybody would be getting the same answers and there would be no competitive advantage to it.

Businesses need to incorporate their marketing data into all of their other data to make sense of it as part of the whole picture of business health. Kemp concedes that 'It's really, really difficult to take everything that's available and do a proper A/B test on it. I'm not saying it's impossible, but the reality is marketers just don't have the patience or the wherewithal to do that most of the time.'

So the competitive advantage once again is curiosity – if you have that then you'll find the patience, you'll find the energy to dig deeper and join the dots between the marketing metrics and what matters to the business.

Avoiding unintended consequences

Kemp shared a story about a client focused on looking at the number of views that a piece of content had received. It was amusing to Kemp that the client decided that the viewer count metric was important 'and guess what the answer was – let's buy a whole lot of ads that increased the view count'. Kemp lamented that all the ads were doing was 'showing it to people that weren't interested, and therefore the conversion rate collapsed and the profitability and everything else was pointless, because the creative hadn't been designed for that audience'.

This is a classic example of a brand getting misguided by using the wrong metric. As Kemp puts it, 'The reason we made that misguided choice was because the powers that be had decided that increasing views was correlated to success.'

I was introduced to the concept of Goodhart's law on my call with Faris and Rosie Yakob. Goodhart's law states that whatever metric you set as a target distorts the system it's designed to serve. So when marketers use a specific metric, this becomes the primary target for decision making and it loses its effectiveness as a useful metric. In other words, if brands focus too much on achieving a specific metric then the pursuit of that number warps behaviour and reduces the metric's ability to reflect true performance. The metric becomes gamed and leads to unintended consequences. Goodhart's law warns marketers that overemphasizing metrics shifts attention away from the underlying business goals they were meant to represent.

What is the real data point?

I'm sorry to say there's more complication – we've seen that we have to measure the right thing and when we measure that thing it may distract us from what we are really trying to do. And what makes it worse is the fact that our individual bonuses and targets can confuse things as well.

I spoke to Executive Creative Director for VaynerMedia Los Angeles, Aaron Howe, who told me he had a client years ago whose compensation was directly tied to how many people called a phone number to sign up for a utility service. The client had instructed Howe to run banner ads on *USA Today*, but without any option to click on the ad – just the phone number was displayed on the ad. The client didn't care about click-through rates; the only thing that mattered was the number of calls, because their bonus was based on that metric. This kind of approach still exists today. He has clients who continue to measure success using outdated methods, like comparing media performance based on traditional TV metrics rather than focusing on social media or digital data. They're often asking the wrong questions or using KPIs that don't reflect what really drives success. It makes sense though – these traditional metrics have shaped their careers, promotions and raises, making them hesitant to shift to more relevant measures.

Howe told me, 'One of the things or the messages I learned… which data supports along with creativity, is really brass tacks, it's kind of like gross to say, but that finding out… your client's compensation, what's it tied to and aligning that, makes such a makes such a huge difference.' This approach, cynical though it is, will steer in a direction that makes the client happy. Knowing whether it's a telephone number on a banner ad, or somebody who is being evaluated on TV metrics, TikToks or they want to get in the press – the happier they are.

There are lessons for us all in this story. Are you currently building someone's bonus or someone's brand? If you're CMO, be careful that you set the right metrics because you may get what you wish for.

Saying 'there's lots of data' doesn't help anyone

Kemp makes the sensible observation that marketing never exists in isolation. Brands may come up with some brilliant new idea but at the same time as the campaign is live there may be some customer service nightmare, the weather might change or a new law might come into play or taxes might increase. Kemp's take is that it's just impossible to isolate marketing in order to give you a clean read on the data. One thing you could do is speak to every individual on every day and ask them why they did the things and hope for a credible and reasonable response, but that is difficult and very unlikely to happen.

In an ideal world you might have a very famous ad like the 1984 Super Bowl advert from Apple which is considered one of the most influential Super Bowl Ads ever,[1] where that was the only thing that they did and there will be an argument that you could attribute everything back to that. Kemp suggests that for most brands this situation is rare and that the average digital marketing campaign has sometimes got tens of thousands of assets. His view in a world where you've got programmatic and dynamic ads is that you simply can't isolate down to a single thing that drove the performance sales brand growth that the brand was after.

Numbers track moments, conversations track emotions

Barbara Galiza insists that we 'take all the data with a grain of salt' and not make decisions on 'faulty data'. In a previous role Galiza worked with a lot of YouTube and influencer content. It was interesting to her that most viewers didn't click on the links and so 'we never really knew how well they were performing'. At the time she was in 'strict negotiations on deals with YouTubers because of what I thought the return on investment was'.

Galiza being Galiza decided to email new users of the product from the last 30 days and asked, 'Where did you find out about us?' It turned out that 25 per cent of users discovered the business via the YouTube content. The data from the clicks in the YouTube ads didn't capture this at all and didn't tell the full story. If you don't ask, you don't get.

Another story she shares was when she was sending emails to lapsed users of a service to try and reactivate them. The open rates of the emails were incredibly low but the numbers of users who came back to the service were way higher than the number of people who opened the email. So the existence of the email in the inbox was enough to trigger people to come back to the business – they didn't even need to open the email. So looking at the numerical data on how many people opened the email was misleading and didn't tell the full story – 'If I had only looked at open rates, I would have no idea what was happening.'

Media data tracks what people did – not what they thought, not what they felt, not what they intended to do or might buy. You have to ask them about that in such a way that you get an honest enough answer because looking at the numerical data alone will tell you much less.

Don't get obsessed with one metric

Peter Field is adamant that 'We should be very wary of simplistic single metrics. Simplistic metrics like that on their own are very unlikely to be right.' His view is that we should take a broad spectrum of metrics like top-of-mind awareness, which he:

> ... would regard as a better one... you have to do the research that teaches you what really influences decision making, and you probably have the model. Sophisticated marketers look at these huge metrics baskets that they gather, and they look for correlations between those metrics, and business results and that's the kind of modelling that you really need to do because then you can not only decide which of those metrics are important, but you can get some sense of the relative importance of them.

Quant vs qual

In my conversation with Meredith Herman she told me that her approach is as follows: 'When I think of the qualitative information, a lot of times we're using that to make sure that we're headed in the right direction, and then you're quantifying that direction with quant to make sure that the depth is there.'

But this is a fine balance and it's easy to get this wrong. Ceci Dones told me, 'I've seen this especially in video where there's "best practices"... the logo must always be in the upper-left-hand corner... we always have to have a call to action on the lower-right-hand corner etc. And because these guidelines exist and data people say "this is the most effective".' Her observation is that this will stifle the creatives who have to make the brand distinct or build a narrative story that isn't necessarily going to end in a call to action: 'When you lean too heavily on the quant side, I find we lose the richness of the qual.'

There's a real danger of being engulfed entirely by quant with an ever-increasing number of ad tech suppliers who will slice and dice every online action into its smallest fraction. The key is not to get overwhelmed by all of the options or obsessed with just one metric. We need to understand what the business problem is, what marketing is trying to achieve and how our metrics are helping us guide us towards a goal that is meaningful, not just to marketing, but to the business.

Data that develops creativity

Field feels very strongly that mental availability is the measure we should all focus on and not get distracted by performance metrics. He asked me, 'How strong is the brand, what is its level of mental availability, how much do people want to buy that brand? Rather than: are they going to do it right now on a click as a result of seeing this piece of performance marketing, which is a very, very different kind of outcome.'

Field believes that the metrics we need to be tracking have to be 'the right kind of effectiveness data'. We need to ask, 'Was it the kind of data that related to long-term effectiveness?' Field's view is that the metrics we track must reflect 'genuine in-market effectiveness, such as market share growth, such as pricing and margin growth and so forth'. Field's take is:

> Those are the kinds of data points that I think really helped develop creativity...
> The problem we've had is that we've had so much data collected that is over a
> very short-term response kind of nature. So, you know, we look at click-based
> kind of data, second-by-second data, and that is really, really misleading. We
> know that that kind of data doesn't relate to genuine long-term sales growth
> and long-term market effectiveness.

Turning people away from brands

The antidote for Field is to 'use long-term data, to look back on our creative work' in order to judge its effectiveness and this is how 'we come to useful conclusions and we will find the right answers to what drives success'. Field reports that 'advertising creativity has been far too driven by performance marketing measures, and I'm afraid I have nothing but criticism for those kinds of performance marketing measures'. The downside of these metrics is that they tell brands 'to get your message in in the first three seconds and you gotta get your brand right there in their faces and you really got to repeat and sell sell sell right on and on'. Field laments this kind of advice from performance marketers and passionately insists, 'I'm not making this up... it sounds like a joke... and that of course leads you to the kind of advertising that simply doesn't drive long-term effectiveness and turns people away from brands.'

Field is not committed on whether these kinds of pushy messages 'have an impact on the short-term sales effectiveness. But that is very dependent on whether or not what you're trying to sell is a valued brand.' Field's opinion, based on his research, is that building a brand 'isn't going to come from that kind of advertising. It will come from advertising somewhere else in the mix. And it's the "somewhere else in the mix" that we've been ignoring because we've become obsessed by the performance marketing model.'

It's harder for the big advertising platforms to prove the long-term brand impact of their serving ads for brands and much easier for them to prove that some clicks happened. Elsewhere in this book we've heard about the dangers of overemphasizing the importance of the data that is easy to get hold of. And it's human nature to underestimate the importance of data that is harder to come by and even deny its existence entirely.

I agree with Field that there is a tendency to over-inflate the importance of performance advertising at times. However, as Lisa Calvino told us, marketing people may define an ad as a 'performance' ad, but to a consumer that performance ad that was meant to drive a sale may be making them 'aware' of that product for the first time. And this, coupled with the fact that many consumers are moving away from traditional storytelling mediums like TV, creates a place where brands need to make short-form ads to have some kind of brand impact. My view is that we need to use the abundant and easy-to-find performance data to learn more about which creative triggers drive attention. Once you have the consumer's attention on the right creative you'll build mental availability, which Field believes is the critical metric for brand building.

Field continues:

> So let's be clear about what mental availability is. It is simplistically described as the extent to which our brand comes to mind in the purchase situation... I'm about to make a purchase of a particular product or service – which brand most immediately floods to mind? It's not simply a question of brand awareness; a lot of people would rather amateurishly describe this as brand awareness but it's actually a relatively unimportant part of it for most brands.

This is an important point – do your target consumers think about your brand when they are in the purchase situation or are they just 'aware' your brand exists? A person could be totally aware that Coke exists but not have the brand come to mind at the moment they want to buy a fizzy drink.

Are performance ads actually performing?

Field believes this is so important to understand because he sees the industry has 'been going the wrong way'. And that brands are reacting to short-term immediate responses to 'in-your-face ads' and that 'we've been walking away from what builds strong brands, we've been walking away from collecting the kind of data that measures strong brands.

'They're in people's minds, how memorable are they, you know, how influential are they over the long term and that requires a different kind of data to the performance marketing and clickstream kind of rubbish that we've been using for the last decade or so to shape advertising.'

Field believes this kind of thinking has infiltrated the boardroom, including the CEOs and CFOs who 'have been seduced by the full certainty of their performance marketing model. Because it's so much more easy to measure... I serve an ad to someone and within a few seconds, I either generate a sale or some kind of response to that I can measure it or I don't, and that seems very certain, of course, you know, the attribution is the key issue here.'

Field asks if it was the performance ad itself that drove that outcome or was it 'actually because of all the work that had been done in the months and years that preceded all of that to convince the consumer or to sell the consumer the value of the brand... of course, we know that most of the work was done in advance and not done by that performance (ad), that's the truth of it... but it's so seductive.'

It's all about the balance

In Field's mind, performance marketing 'seems very certain' but in fact performance ads 'are misleading because the numbers we're working with in this supposedly certain world of performance marketing are anything but certain'. How we attribute a sale to which ad is a 'big issue because so much of the effectiveness of that performance marketing is actually predicated on the strength of the brand that you're trying to build'.

It's an uncomfortable truth for suppliers who trade purely in performance ads because, as Field puts it, 'That performance marketing dollar will work a damn sight harder if we've also spent a whole load of dollars in the background building the brand – and we know that we absolutely know that 110 per cent.'

Field reports that 'There is a huge fallacy in the apparent certainty of this and that has been sold in not just to marketers, but to their bosses by the big digital platforms... who have been preaching this mantra of accountability and certainty to CEOs and CFOs and they love all of that.' But it's not all over, far from it. Field reassures us by saying, 'The long and the short of it is to say that there are two sides to effectiveness long term.' Brands need to balance the need for short-term performance results with the steady progress of brand building over time, and 'You have to do both and you have to do them in some kind of balance'.

This last line quote is central to Field's view (he co-wrote a book about it). His interview was one of the most powerful I undertook in this research. Field is a fierce advocate that performance and brand are powerful together as combined ingredients and not dishes in their right. However, it's worth looking at your own organization and asking yourself if your brand and performance teams communicate well, are in the same time zone, country, building, office or at least mindset. Or are they kept at arm's length as they sneer and spit in disdain at each other's uncomfortable and unattractive differences?

2.5 seconds to go

Field is interested in the data that's coming out of companies like Amplified Intelligence that looks at the duration of people's active attention on ads from different video ad platforms. Metrics that capture the amount of attention an ad receives are important when considering the findings of a key study done by Karen Nelson Field. Peter Field rates his namesake as 'one of the pioneers of the attention revolution. What she has learned from her study… is that you need at least two-and-a-half seconds… of attention (on a video ad) before we can form the kind of memory structures that will drive long-term effectiveness and build mental availability.'

As mentioned earlier, mental availability is a metric that captures if a brand comes to mind at the point of purchase. So it takes a two-and-a-half-second view of video (as a minimum) to start to build mental availability. Field continues, 'Actually, it's an exponential response curve. And if we can get to 10 seconds of attention, we have a massively bigger impact than if we only just achieve two-and-a-half seconds.'

Why do your ads capture attention?

Field talks about when 130,000 views of digital ads were studied, only 15 per cent of them met the attention threshold to build mental availability and 'only a handful met the 10 second threshold, which I would regard as a proper storytelling period of time.' The harsh truth is that 'most digital platforms and Facebook… for instance, its average is somewhere around about one second of active eyes on attention. So you ain't never going to build a brand on that kind of platform.' In Field's view it's true that brands 'can use it for performance very powerfully. You might be able to use it to remind people to nudge a memory of brand-building work they have seen else-where, such as on TV, but you're not going to build a brand on that particular platform.'

My view is that all seconds of attention are not equal and though Nelson Field's work gives us a guide for what we should be aiming for, the content of each of those seconds makes a huge and often immeasurable difference. We've been making digital ads that capture attention at Automated Creative for a long time and we've seen that brands need to focus on making sure that the start of their video content is exciting enough to keep people engaged to watch the rest of the video. It's our practice of testing multiple versions of the start of a video to see what stops people scrolling. Most brands would kill to get to 10 seconds of attention; in fact two-and-a-half would please most, but first brands need to stop consumers in their tracks and keep their attention on the brands you represent. This is done by testing and learning, working out which video elements work for which audiences. It's not as simple as getting two-and-a-half seconds of attention, it's under-standing *why* your creative captured their attention.

Field continues his point:

> You've got to appreciate and understand how the two (brand/performance) work together, so collect the right data, look for the right patterns, ensure that you are clear in your mind about what you're doing to build the brand versus what you're doing to drive short-term sales now in performance marketing, and those two kinds of creativity will look very different.

The industry is awash with people who are keen to say 'it depends' when brands ask for advice and that's fair – all products are different in some way and each audience has different needs. But Field is passionate on this point that he sees as applying to most of us:

> We can't walk away from story building as the essence of brand building – it's the essence of effectiveness. We've just got to learn how to do it within the constraints imposed on us by many but not all digital platforms. These kinds of short-term engagement-type metrics may be free or cheap or very easy to measure but they have zero value, frankly, to long term.

Getting the attribution right

When Field talks about getting the right data and looking for the right patterns he advises that we 'use modelling techniques, long-term market mix modelling, econometric modelling, as we want to call it, that can actually look much more reliably at attribution'. One practitioner who has done this successfully is Brompton Bike's Lisa Calvino, who told me:

> We've recently implemented multi-touch attribution (MTA) reporting, so we've moved away from last click. And before implementing this, we were ready to pause bidding on generic terms, so things like 'folding bikes' for various reasons, but the CPCs were high, conversions were low, and our ROAS was negative, but implementing MTA has enabled us to see the full story.'

Calvino continues, 'We were all ready to switch it [bidding on generic keywords like folding bikes] off, because the way we were reporting was suggesting it wasn't profitable. It just wasn't really having any impact, not necessarily a negative one, but just any impact.' Calvino dug into her MTA data and noticed it 'was really showing us what was driving that first kind of click – were they coming to us through that ad? It then meant that we could feel a bit more confident in that generic strategy from a search point of view. So we've then started to just build that out.'

Calvino specifically told me that she 'started at very basic terms like "folding bikes" then started to build that out and test longer-tail variations. So when people are looking for "best commuter bikes"... there are other things that we then need to start testing.' The interesting insight here is that consumers 'might not know that they're looking for a folding bike at that point' but Calvino's team need to look at all of the signs they're indicating that they're open to a folding bike.

Calvino told me:

> Having this way of reporting and understanding how important it is to get in front of those users before they know that they're looking for it is really key for us, because that's the only way we're going to grow as a business – if we convert more people that don't know that they need a folding bike.

Calvino's use of MTA has 'enabled us to see the full journey. So whilst people didn't convert on the term "folding bike" – obviously no one's just typing "folding bike" and then purchasing right there... that was then the start of their research journey.' Calvino's next step was to get in front of those users early and then 'We were then able to retarget and be front of their mind throughout their journey. So the MTA proved that the ROAS was profitable... so we didn't switch off and then we instead, we scaled our spend, so that resulted in growth to our top-line revenue.'

If Calvino had only looked at her paid search data which didn't show any profitability the brand would have turned off bidding against generic terms.

This would have cost the business money and 'We would have thought we were doing the right thing... but we wouldn't be then getting in front of new users who were just at the start of that journey. So that was really telling, because we were, like, absolutely ready to switch that off and kind of save that money. So for us, that was quite a big turning point.'

Being engaged doesn't mean you're committed

Another metric that has been popular in the pursuit of data-driven marketing has been 'engagement' but it's not without its issues, as Lex Bradshaw-Zanger told me in our interview:

> There's an obsession in the digital world around engagement rates. I remember
> at Facebook... this was a long time ago that we had this Nielsen chart that said
> there is no correlation between engagement and business results because there
> are people who don't want to click on ads, people who don't want to comment
> and like.

Bradshaw-Zanger's take is:

> Relative engagement rates are a signal of the strength of creativity... to videos
> to static ads... one's got more likes than another. That is a relative signal of the
> performer to the creativity. So I think that's super important. And then we start
> to look at more metrics like viewability and attention and these sorts of things.
> We use AI to look at some of our more performance-driven work to see where
> eye tracking is going in this sort of thing. So there's loads of data points now that
> start to help you optimize pre-flight and in-flight analysis – I don't know if that
> helps you on the creativity per se, but it's definitely how you optimize creative.

So looking at engagement rates as a 'relative signal' is useful – it's not perfect but no single data point is. If it works for you, double down on it but first you need to be honest about what the data is telling you.

Matt Cosad's take on tracking engagement is that 'If you focus on engagement metrics, and then you push ads, and then you look at engagement, a lot of what I've seen happen in the past at other places I've worked is that you'll start comparing this campaign to a previous campaign and you want to do a little bit incrementally better.' This will seem sensible to most marketers but Cosad continues:

> It's very hard to get honest stretch targets in place; people always put in
> benchmarks and make it look like they're doing better than they have in the past.
>
> If you compare the realistic target for engagement... that's kind of the
> missing piece of the puzzle... people will say 'Oh, I got a 5 per cent engagement
> rate on this post, it's incredible' but if you look like at creators that people really

want to follow, like Mr. Beast, for example, they're gonna get somewhere like 40 or 50 or 60 per cent engagement with their stuff. You're getting 6 per cent this year, when it was 5 per cent last year and considering that you're successful on the platform, it's just completely misguided, right?

Cosad continues that brands need to say 'We're just going to stand in the same arena as people who are authentically interesting and that people want to follow – and we're going to go up against them. And we're going to try and compete for people's attention metrics that represent that sort of ambition.' This is a whopping goal and one that I've not come across from a brand marketer, but I completely back this – have the ambition to be the best, not follow best practice.

Organic metrics

Cosad said that while he was at Heinz he found growing an organic following very difficult. His provocation to marketers is to ask:

> Are regular people going to follow this [brand account] without knowing that they're going to get offers, are they going to follow it without thinking there's going to be deals or discounts or anything of that sort? Do they actually just want to consume our content? This is a really important question. And I think it's something that a lot of brands don't necessarily get right. They just tend to take ad formats and just push them out to all the different channels they have like a digital extension of their TV campaign and cut downs. Like everybody knows, it isn't really best practice, but it doesn't stop people from doing it.

I wish I could say I'd seen evidence to the contrary but the opposite of data-driven marketing is to take the TV creative and squish it into other types of media. It can be convenient and save money on creative and production costs to do that and might make sense to the board. But you won't be being curious, which is the key to getting data and creativity right. A little curiosity about your audience will tell you that they go to other channels for different reasons than they watch TV.

Brand is performance and performance is brand

Calvino told me:

> We've gone from last year where we had a brand budget and a performance budget, or an 'ecom budget'. We've merged those this year to say they're all

doing the same thing, but we're not attributing one to brand awareness and one to ecom. Because it's so hard to split purely from a paperwork point of view, it was messy... If someone coming across it [an ad] for the first time, that's an 'awareness' point of view but if that's someone coming across it for the fifth time, and they've already been in store and they've considered and that [ad] tips them over the edge, but it's the same ad... So I think everything now is full funnel... unless you've got a conversion driving coupon, you've retargeted them because they've added to basket, but haven't converted in a week – then I think everything is a full-funnel ad.

This view does not sit nicely with the way a lot of the organizations I know are set up. And it will be uncomfortable because it's right. The way we set our campaigns up and what we want them to do will clash with the reality of a messy, chaotic and impulse-driven consumer who doesn't care in even the most miniscule way whether our ads were intended to be 'awareness' or 'performance' in nature.

The cost of acquiring new customers has to go up, not down

It's time for some more uncomfortable truths about data-driven marketing. A lot of the performance marketing industry is tasked with reducing the cost-per-acquisition of a new customer. If we can get people to buy our product for an increasingly lower cost to the business then everyone is happy. It's a metric that everyone from the CEO to the car park attendant can get their head around. If only marketing were this simple.

Galiza shared her thoughts with me on the magical CPA metric. Her view is that a big focus of data-driven marketing is the holy grail of driving down the cost-per-acquisition of new customers. This is intended to happen from adverts that consumers are meant to click on and then complete a purchase shortly after. If you can lower the CPA, everyone is happy – it means the whole thing is working together beautifully. Not for Galiza.

In her view, the bigger that the audience gets, then the more education (or ads) the audience will need in order to convert them to being a customer. And the more education that is needed means more money spent and this results in a higher CPA.

In Galiza's words, 'It's the absolute nature of performance marketing that the CPAs will go up because you're reaching people that are more difficult to convert.' If your market is constantly expanding then this is avoidable, but if your brand's growth ambitions are to grow at a faster pace than the market of people that will buy from you with little education, then you'll have to cast a wider net and spend more money to convert these potential customers. The goal for Galiza isn't to lose sight of what is important by being fixated on CPA. Her focus is to find the customers who spend regularly with you and stay with you for longer. And to learn from their signals and get a better understanding of what they want. That's the value to the business, not just the cost of getting them through the door.

I've met countless brand teams and performance teams over the last 17 years but very few (if any) 'retention' teams. Galiza's advice is to not get distracted about the immediate and satisfying feeling of completing a sale but the long and relentless job of keeping customers so happy they keep coming back.

The most common refrain in all of my research was 'there's so much data', as if it's some Herculean test of the modern marketer even to comprehend it. I think this stems from the idea that there is some value in all data somewhere and if we ignore some of it we are willingly ignoring value and not doing our jobs.

Basket of data

No one data point will tell you everything you need to know. If we point an organization towards a singular data point then that data point could start to work against us. It's human nature to game a system and want to thrive so serving one data point is not enough. Rosie Yakob says what we need is 'a basket of data, looking to gather insight into what could help us make decisions about the next creative campaign'. The thing to do here is to understand what business problem marketing is trying to solve and collate all your meaningful marketing metrics into one place. Then you need to get rid of all of the data points that are not going to help you make an informed decision about what creative and media decisions to make next. Yakob states, 'Don't measure things unless they are going to help you make a decision. What decisions do we need to make and what data points will help us make those decisions?'

We need to beware the 'interesting' trap. If it's interesting that you have a click-through rate of 5 per cent but it's not going to make any new decisions based on it then ignore it, it's just interesting. What are the basket of data points that are going to help make your next campaign better than the last? Everything else is a distraction.

Field goes one step further and says, 'You've got to be quite clear about what are the basket of individual metrics that will make up mental availability, and it will vary hugely from one category to another.' So whether you're after mental availability or another consumer outcome, get the right metrics all in one place and refine as you go.

Summary of metrics

It's easier to measure if someone sees an ad, clicks on it and buys something. But this doesn't tell us what the impact of previous brand messaging on any platform had on that click. Brand and performance ads are not distinct in their impact, only their intent.

To effectively use data in marketing, metrics must align with broader business objectives rather than serving our much-loved marketing KPIs. Let's use data to direct us and not dictate, and if metrics don't grow the business they can mislead teams into chasing superficial wins. Rather than over-relying on a single metric, a balanced 'basket of data' provides a fuller picture, capturing both short-term performance and long-term brand health.

Finally, it's important to remain critical and honest about what data can and cannot reveal. Metrics typically capture an event that happened but often miss the motivations and emotions driving those actions. Integrating qualitative insights with quantitative data provides a richer understanding of consumer behaviour. This balanced approach – using data to guide decisions while trying to capture an audience's gooey feelings and preferences – puts you in a position to be data guided and emotionally grounded.

Briefs build on insight

Your creative brief can either inspire your creatives or confuse them. Here's exactly how you distil a ton of data into an inspiring brief that actually gets great work out the other end.

Writing a creative brief is one of the most important steps in advertising. In this chapter, we'll explore how data can inform the brief so that the resulting work is clear, focused and creatively inspiring. As Jon Williams says, 'Data will inform a brief, and a well-informed brief creates the best work.' But data alone can't guarantee a good creative brief. It's 'how you articulate it (data) in a creative, interesting and inspiring way that will lead to more creativity down the line,' explains Rosie Yakob.

Historically, many ad agencies have attempted to shield creatives from looking at reams of spreadsheets, leaving planners to figure out what the data means and then serve up that understanding in a succinct creative brief. Faris Yakob recalls the traditional approach: 'No data for creatives, they never see it, never gonna look at it. They may see a creative brief with an insight in it, they may involve data. But you're not asking creatives to go through reams of spreadsheets.' This ensures that creatives focus on the ideation side, while planners carry the burden of turning data into something useful to the creative process. When data is successfully translated, it becomes a source of insights that creatives can use to solve the underlying business problem.

Strategy as sacrifice

At the heart of all data-informed creativity is strategy. Kemp's view is that 'strategy is the art of sacrifice'. He believes marketers today face endless possibilities, so the trick is to narrow down those options and then act confidently, deciding that what remains is the best course of action. Kemp also warns us to use data to ensure we're asking the right questions – 'Because a brilliant answer to the wrong question is still worthless,' he says. By focusing on the right questions, you avoid wasted creative energy and can zero in on the best opportunity. Kemp's method for developing strategy is straightforward: first, work out what you need to do, then figure out why it's difficult, and finally, ask why you haven't already done it before. That sequence can reveal what steps remain and guide you in planning your journey. The underlying point is that data helps illuminate who the right audience is, where they are, and what mindset they're in, before starting to formulate creative ideas.

Data gives direction

When asked how we can use data to create ads that are emotionally resonant, funny, or that endure and position brands favourably, Kemp's response is that 'you actually can't, but you can improve your chances'. Data can't reliably promise comedic genius or universal emotional appeal but it can help ensure that you're targeting the right audience in the right context. When you know what people care about, where they are and what resonates with them, the odds of producing effective creative improve. Kemp's view is that data alone doesn't conjure the brilliant idea, but it can point you in the right direction.

The brief should reveal your target

The best briefs are often the ones that don't forget that real humans will see the ad. That's a principle Perla Bloom, ex Global Strategy Lead at EA Entertainment, lives by. She tells a story from her work on a financial services brand, specifically a campaign to promote a digital 'kitty' where groups can contribute money into the same pot. Bloom's job was to brief creatives to turn what she describes as 'a pretty stale' proposition into something fun and interesting.

On top of that, she faced the strategic challenge of identifying an insight that worked across various global markets, all of which had different cultural attitudes towards money. Bloom realized that typical industry reports wouldn't go far enough, so she dug into psychological and societal academic papers to find universal truths, especially around the social awkwardness of handling money with friends.

That discovery gave the creative team 'a great springboard for some ideas that were really going to connect with people and their relationships with people and money, to make that kind of stale product relevant to people in their day-to-day lives'. She notes how sometimes you need to think beyond the data in front of you and expand outward: 'You have to think outside the box a little bit of what you're researching and what you're inputting.'

Once she pinned down the insight, she tested, or 'falsified' it, pulling in first-party data, cultural references and cross-functional feedback. Bloom's goal is to accurately represent the consumer. It's her job to 'act as the bridge between the breadth of data and the insight but ultimately to represent the person who's going to see the ad,' she says. Her mission is to 'bridge the gap between what we need the consumer to do, and something that's actually going to make them do it'.

An insight should never be fully surprising

One of the biggest obstacles is bridging the gap between the data, marketing people and creative people. There can be a mismatch of their languages and objectives. The data teams focus on precision and proof, while creative teams want emotive resonance and narrative potential, and the marketing contingent might be pressing to solve immediate business needs. Bloom argues that a strong insight overcomes this divide. Her view is that an insight should actually connect with people and bridge the gap between data and a creative execution. The goal is to have a solid insight that really is that 'aha' moment: 'An insight should never be something that fully surprises people – it should be a real behavioural truth, but it should be said in a way that they've never heard before.'

Don't overload the brief

A recurring theme is the caution not to bury the creative team with too much data. Creatives like Becky McOwen-Banks say that there is a tendency to overload briefs with evidence, but the real power lies in the clarity of the simple message. Tash Beecher agrees, referencing what she calls 'a palatable, human truth'. If the strategy team feeds too many facts into the brief, it can lose focus. Bloom, though she loves data, understands the pitfall of giving creatives too many data points to interpret without pointing to a single insight. Too many details can muddle the spark that helps creatives see a path to big ideas. So the simpler the brief, the more direct the insight, the more likely the creative solution will resonate.

The difference between a data point and an insight

Bloom helpfully articulated the difference between a data point and an insight to me: 'A data point is a *fact* – a one-dimensional descriptive piece of information.' By contrast, an insight 'should *inspire* action. It has to represent culture, the audience and the product/brand.' A lonely data point can be mistaken for an insight, which can prompt teams to fixate on the wrong thing. Bloom argues that an insight should connect dots in a way that spurs creative possibility and yields real business impact. She's also seen situations where different teams latch onto separate data points and treat them as insights, thereby causing conflict. 'An insight,' she emphasizes, 'should be something that makes the pit of a creative's stomach set alight and make them want to create.' That's the difference. If it doesn't spark excitement or an 'aha' moment, it's probably just a piece of data, not an insight.

REAL-WORLD EXAMPLES
EA's Wild Hearts, British Airways and teeth whitening

EA

A clear demonstration of Bloom's thinking comes from the strategy for EA's beast-hunting game Wild Hearts. The game immerses you in an organic, beautiful wilderness where you chase hybrid creatures – half beast, half nature. There's a duality, as the player admires nature's beauty but also uses technology to slay beasts that are part nature themselves. Bloom's objective was to make a niche 'hunter game' appealing to an audience outside of that category. She decided to connect the game to cultural sentiments about nature and our modern world. The data point she surfaced was that around 50 per cent of people are worried about global warming and the negativity surrounding environmental crises, yet there's also a sense of fascination with how nature can inspire solutions, from new therapies to design ideas. Bloom's insight latched onto this interplay of nature and technology, tapping into the awe people feel when these two forces converge. That's the heart of the creative pivot: connect the 'hunter game' with the universal curiosity humans have about nature's power and the possibilities of technology.

Sometimes an insight emerges from a systematic approach to data, and sometimes it starts with an offhand comment or random observation. Sam Gaunt says, 'It's about a series of hypotheses, and sometimes those hypotheses can be generated from the data. But sometimes that hypothesis might just come from a conversation in the pub, or walking the dog.' Gaunt believes anyone can take two facts, connect them and propose a hypothesis for a campaign or strategy, but the real skill is in testing, refining and verifying whether it truly stands as an insight. Lucy Jameson talks about 'finding a glitch in the matrix', that moment something in the data or the culture doesn't align with your expectations. That is often a goldmine for insights.

British Airways: the British original

A prime illustration of translating hypothesis and pattern recognition into brand positioning can be seen in the story of British Airways. The pitch team came up with 'A British Original', in contrast to the previous claim of 'made in Britain'. Jameson admitted to being unsure what 'made in Britain' signified in modern times. So they scoured every platform and conversation to see what contemporary Britishness truly means. The pattern they identified was that Britain still exerts a form of 'soft power' through creativity, originality, music, the arts and invention. Stormzy and the creation of new vaccines both sit on the same continuum of British inventiveness. They recognized that the outdated colonial connotations might not resonate with a global audience, so they pivoted to celebrating a different, more inclusive sense of Britishness. That's how 'A British Original' was born. Jameson refers to pattern recognition as the key skill, spotting something unexpected or noticing why a phenomenon doesn't play out as you'd predict. That can spark a brand's entire new positioning.

Looking at teeth whitening

Jameson offers another anecdote about working on a teeth sensitivity campaign. Conventional logic would focus on dentist recommendations, but Jameson noticed something else: the rise of teeth whitening procedures, which can cause increased sensitivity. By connecting the data around whitening treatments with sensitivity pains, the conversation shifts to 'the price of beauty'. It broadens the creative territory from a purely functional claim of dentist approval to an emotionally rich space about societal pressure, vanity and self-care. Suddenly, the campaign conversation becomes more interesting and layered.

Beware the data

Not everyone is sold on how data leads directly to great insights. Field says, 'I think I'm still profoundly disappointed with the way people use data to generate insights. It has huge and interesting potential, but it's pretty rare where I see insights that have led to great creativity that have come directly from data.' In his experience, data rarely leaps off the page and into a big idea without interpretation and contextualization. Bloom also warns that 'just because the idea is entrenched in data doesn't mean it's good necessarily'. She's seen how data can end up suffocating creativity if used incorrectly, or become a weapon to force approval on half-baked ideas.

BEING DATA-INFORMED, NOT DATA-CONSTRAINED

When I interviewed Bloom, she was Global Strategy Lead at EA Entertainment. Her role put her at the centre of creativity and data, pulling them together to sing in harmony to launch new gaming titles. Her experience in bringing together creativity and data is far from theoretical. It was her role to get the right kind of data and intelligence to write a brief for her creative teams to deliver the business outcomes EA needs. It's her opinion that data isn't an absolute, that it doesn't have any power in its own right and that her goal is that the creative work she inspires is 'being data-informed versus data-constrained'. Data isn't a validation but a springboard for new creative greatness. She sees using data with creativity as a superpower: 'Bringing together data and creativity doesn't make it automatically stale and boring. It should make us branch out to places that we've never even thought about.' Bloom embraces the unhinged nature of creativity: 'There's always going to be an element of unpredictability and creativity and that's something that is not going to be taken away with data… (it) breeds a more fertile ground.'

Her message is that data can release untapped power in creativity but it can be used as a stick to beat creativity with or falsely prop it up. The problem for Bloom is that without data we are limiting creativity to the world view of the creative person coming up with the ideas. Also, it is possible to use data to stifle creativity – 'If it was completely reliant on data, it would not be creativity' – and it's also possible to use data to prove the rightness of the wrong idea.

Respecting the audience

One of the recurring insights is that your brief should speak for the consumer, the viewer, the player – whoever the ultimate audience may be. Bloom insists on starting with their perspective: 'Your brief should represent the person that's going to see the ad.' If the data reveals a cultural tension, a recognizable awkwardness or an unmet need, that's when a creative team can build something that might just capture someone's attention. Using a single statistic or fact as the entire basis for creativity without anchoring it in audience reality is a missed opportunity. Instead, a truly data-informed brief pulls together facts, behaviours, cultural context and the truth about a brand into a catalytic insight that creative teams can get behind.

A model for data, creativity and advertising

Throughout these anecdotes and examples, a loose framework emerges for using data effectively in creative briefs. First, define the business challenge or objective. Second, use data to shine a light on the audience and the relevant truths about their behaviour or culture. Third, define a unifying insight that resonates emotionally, something that creates excitement. Fourth, keep the brief simple – avoid drowning the creative team in facts. Fifth, validate or falsify that insight with multiple data sources, ensuring it's robust. Finally, recognize that creativity thrives on a bit of unpredictability. Let the data direct you to fertile pastures but don't let it dictate the final creative idea. That is how you remain data-informed rather than data-constrained.

Summary

In writing a creative brief with data, we need to recognize that the role of data is to guide, not to overshadow. As these interviews have emphasized, data will inform a brief, and a well-informed brief creates the best work, but the real magic happens when data is turned into a potent insight that bridges the gap between business needs and genuine human truths. Kemp's belief that strategy involves sacrifice reminds us that focusing on the right question is everything.

Bloom's method of delving into psychological, societal and cultural academic papers demonstrates how wide and deep you sometimes need to go to find a real universal truth. Once that truth is found, it's tested, refined and presented in a way that sparks excitement among creatives. Whether it's for a financial services brand or a beast-hunting game with environmental undertones, the principle remains the same.

The job of the strategist or planner is to represent the people who will see the ad. By bridging the gap between data and creativity, the creative brief inspires creative excitement, not becoming a straitjacket for ideas. It points the team towards a solution that resonates emotionally and culturally. Bloom's recognition that data can stifle creativity if misapplied should serve as an important reminder. If you rely on data purely for validation, you may find yourself pushing forward ideas you're not proud of. But when you use data as a springboard, a hypothesis generator and a directional guide, you get briefs that excite the creatives.

In the end, the trick to writing a data-informed creative brief is to find that sweet spot: present the data with clarity, revolve it around a simple, universal insight and give the creative mind a chance to produce ideas that break the category codes and surprise our audiences.

KEY TAKEAWAYS

- Measure only what you will act upon.
- Watch out for metrics that just make you look good but nothing else.
- Use qualitative insights to reveal the true story behind your numbers.
- Briefs should be stupidly simple and inspiring – ditch the decks.
- A data point is just a fact. An insight makes a creative want to hug you.
- Less data, more clarity. Your team will thank you.

Note

1   Austerlitz, S (2024) 40 years ago, this ad changed the Super Bowl forever, *The New York Times*, 9 Feb, www.nytimes.com/2024/02/09/arts/television/super-bowl-apple-1984-ad.html (archived at https://perma.cc/MML5-PGPH)

10

The art of standing out

This chapter talks about how data can inspire better ideas without draining the life out of creativity.

I really hate the word ideation, but I admit that I've used it a lot. It's one of those words that show us how disconnected advertising is from real people. I've never said, 'I had a great ideation session the other day' to my real friends. And it can get even worse. I heard someone at a conference in London say that their agency does 'imagineering' – I nearly spat out my coffee. The ad industry loves a portmanteau and an acronym to make something simple sound cleverer than it is.

Despite the ad industry's penchant for complicating simple things, ideas for most remain the most exciting part of the business. It's often what draws us into this profession – it certainly did me. Where else can you get paid to combine science, data, psychology and art to come up with ideas that move people? Great ideas that drive business value are rare, so much so that great creativity is the exception and not the rule. So how do you tap into the parallel universe of ideas that surprise and stand out? This chapter shares the wisdom of some incredibly experienced folk who have used data to make this happen.

The most interesting thing about creativity is its ability to seemingly come from nowhere and delight us. Perhaps you are the kind of person who doesn't see themselves as a creative person but everyone has had ideas that appeared out of nowhere. Ideas that surprised us that have unknown origins in the dark recesses of our brains. Most of us won't have 'creative' in our job title but we can use the advice below to help better ideas happen more often. As Perla Bloom puts it, 'There's always going to be an element of unpredictability and creativity and that's something that is not going to be taken away with data.' Her take is that data 'breeds a more fertile ground' for creativity to happen.

This chapter explores how data and creativity collide in that moment of inspiration; how some of the smartest minds in the industry harness data to fuel ideas that don't just blend in, but demand attention.

Creativity as insubordination

It's human nature to want to spot patterns and copy others. It's common to be praised for fitting in and for following the rules but this is a disadvantage in advertising. It's our job to make brands stand out and buck the trend. As Rory Sutherland puts it, 'Every act of creativity can be interpreted as an act of insubordination.' We must embrace creative talent and understand that 'Creative people don't start work straight away. They actually question the question. They question the brief. They're massive procrastinators. They wait to get lucky. They become tangential. They go off at tangents. They have no sense of proportion.' The ideas that work should 'look like insubordination and bad behaviour within an institution'. This is our goal, to break the rules, buck the trend and embrace the weird – and data can help us get there.

Data won't solve a creative problem

Simon Kemp echoes Sutherland's thoughts that questions need to be questioned. The key step here is asking the questions we need to ask in order to start analysing what the correct data sources are. Once we have the correct data sources, then we have the foundations of what might be an audience, what might be a behaviour, and then we start thinking about what might be a platform. And that is the point when the data has done its job and the creativity begins.

Despite being one of the most data-centric advertising people there is, Kemp's belief is that data will never give you an answer to a creative problem. His view is that this would be a bit like 'looking for alchemy – but good luck finding it'. Kemp's view is that data isn't the light bulb going on but the electricity going into the lightbulb – marketers still need to flip the switch.

Don't let the data drive it too much

Tom Goodwin's take is that historically, the advertising industry was very resistant to using data to inform the creative process. There was a sense that data was the 'enemy' and that using data would undermine the ability to create great, intuitive ads. Goodwin acknowledges that there is a place for data in the creative process but argues that data should not be the sole driver. He believes data should be used to support and inform decisions, rather than to dictate the entire creative direction.

Goodwin recounts how the movie industry uses data-driven insights, like knowing a film shouldn't be too long or too short, without explicitly labelling it as 'data'. Instead, it's considered common sense or instinct. Goodwin argues that the advertising industry has swung too far in the direction of relying solely on data, with some companies using data to make overly prescriptive creative decisions. He believes this approach stifles true creativity.

Goodwin advocates for a balanced approach that combines data-driven insights with creative instinct and expertise, using data to support and optimize the creative process rather than to dictate it entirely.

Start with a hunch

But how do you actually do this? Well it's not easy but Lisa Calvino says, 'You need to be able to test things without any data to start with. You want to have a hunch, and actually, that hunch should be based off of something that isn't ego, and I guess that that's the hard bit to decipher where it's coming from.' It's an uncomfortable truth that it's hard to predict where a good idea will come from and how. One solution for a brand has been to conform to what lots of other brands have done in the past in the hope that what has worked previously will do so again in the future. This approach, though common, is flawed.

To put this simply, imagine a market with a row of stalls selling fruit. One day the first stall sells more products than the others. The other fruit sellers gather around and agree 'best practice' is to do what the top seller has done. The next day all the other stalls copy the top-selling stall in terms of how it looks, prices, salespeople etc. This is the opposite of standing out from the market (which is what marketing is) – it's purely fitting in. But yet this practice is prevalent.

Data is the darling of the risk averse

Lucy Jameson says that when she is looking at best practice advice from the big ad platforms it 'makes me want to shoot myself, because it is really boring'. She baulks at the aggregate suggestion that you should 'shove the bloody brand logo at the beginning' as this crushes creativity and makes it 'hard to know how you do anything interesting.' The end result is that the industry is forced into making ads that feel 'just a bit wallpaper to me. So I do struggle with kind of figuring out how to approach that in a more interesting way.'

This is one of the downsides of data – it acts as a protector. Data is the darling of the risk averse. As Jameson puts it, 'Sometimes you're just never gonna convince some people to be the person who puts their head above the parapet and something different because then they're at risk of failing and then losing their job. They're safe.' It's true that someone who follows the creative codes of the past won't get fired for it but as Jameson says, 'They're not going to do much'.

Becky McOwen-Banks' view is that at a certain point creativity needs to be set free to do its thing and not be trapped by the constraints of data. Data is great for learning and evaluation but all of that 'should have fed that into the human brain or whatever it is beforehand'. Unfortunately sometimes the data-obsessed will say we can't explore a previously explored avenue, 'because we've been there before, and that didn't work, or you can't move that way because so and so said that the other brand that is similar to us did that, and they didn't like that at all'. In the act of creation, you have to be without those constraints of data or you will 'end up in a position where you can't move'. Once the creative is deployed then the smart thing is to use data to evaluate, learn and adapt.

Matt Cosad takes this further, saying that following the big ad platforms' best practices means a lot of the time he 'ends up producing content that doesn't really stand out in any way'. And standing out is our job as marketers, not copying. Cosad told me, 'Those platform best practices will end up producing content that always feels very similar.' And this is a bad place to be – if your brand looks and acts like everyone else, you're toast. Be bold, be different, be noticed or, as Cosad remarks, you're just going to fit into a 'single algorithmic view of what is good-quality creative, and it's going to just reduce the quality of what's going out'. And this is coming from someone who has been at the coalface of making creativity work for one of marketing's most revered brands – Heinz.

Cosad continues that he's been struggling over the past four years or so to create good 'quality creative without obsessing over the numbers too much' and his realization was that 'We've never been able to make successful campaigns by numbers.' The reason for this is that Cosad's numbers meant that his team 'weren't looking at the full picture. And as a result, we were drawing out the wrong insights.' Cosad's perception is that most people in the industry would say that it's impossible to capture the magic of creative with numbers, to which he says, 'I don't know whether that's true or not.' He's unsure if this will change in the future. But he is frank that 'Until recently the tools we were using to diagnose creative performance with analytics weren't able to capture the full picture. So we weren't doing analysis on the right stuff.'

You can have all the opinions you like but not all of us have had years of trying to make creative and data work like Cosad. And his view that data doesn't capture the full picture is vital when we approach making data and creativity work together. He admits that 'Recognizing that we were missing a lot of the components of creative success was kind of the biggest "aha" moment for me about delivering high-quality creative.'

Aggregate data that comes from the big platforms is an amalgamation of data from other brands often in other sectors in other markets with other audiences and ambitions. This data is 'interesting' but all too often it's not insightful. If data is making you avoid risk you're on the path to sameness; you should be using data to find new ways to take risks. That's where the potential is.

We are speaking to humans (not robots)

According to Peter Field this overreliance on data in the creative process in the last 15 years or so has 'been very disruptive of creativity'. His belief is that the performance marketing industry has a lot to answer for. His take is that 'If you look at the kind of creative work that is increasingly run these days, even when we think we're trying to build brands, it has been heavily influenced by all of that performance marketing thinking that says we got to get in there, we got to sell from second one.'

He sees a move away from the need to 'build seductive storylines and engage consumers emotionally because we've got to get in there and sell' and that the reflex is 'to keep repeating our message in people's faces time and time again'. Alex Jenkins echoes this position by saying that you 'can't just abdicate responsibility to the data. At some point you've got to say. "I don't think I can rationalize it." Because creativity can't always be rationalized. If it could, it probably wouldn't be very creative.'

David Byrne builds on this by saying, 'Data can inform creative, but most distinctive, breakthrough work comes from abstract ideas I would say that defy perceived wisdom, data patterns and category conventions. Gorilla playing the drums for confectionary anyone?'

Our job, as ever, is being empathetic. Our job as marketers isn't to get better click-through rates, it's to communicate the value of a brand's products to the people we want to influence to buy them. Or, as Field puts it, 'Just remember, it's human beings that we're communicating with, not robots.' So do you have data on what your specific audience feels or are you acting on aggregate data from one of the big ad platforms' latest report they sent to everyone else in the hope you'd spend more of your media budget with them?

So what can you do with data in the ideation process?

First of all, not all data comes in 1s and 0s, and Jagdish Sheth suggests that we need to expose ourselves to 'a diverse set of information, magazines, journals online'. His view is that creatives need to use more organic sources of data to become 'a deep generalist' who can spot new connections between the data and get an 'aha moment'. Sheth's point will be obvious to some, but not everyone wants to immerse themselves in a deep pool of content in the hope that tangential synaptic links are formed in the short amount of time clients expect their creative teams to produce advertising gold. Others rely on their strategic-thinking friends. As Tash Beecher puts it, 'As a creative, a planner or your strategist is your best friend.'

Tiffany Rolfe's view is that the strategy team should be 'pulling the right insights that they find to help get to a creative brief'. And that creative folk need to be 'trusting them to kind of find some different territories and areas of expertise based on all of that data and then narrowing in on a few different directions'. Once the map has been laid out it's up to the creative and strategic leadership to get in a room and 'debate'.

Rolfe's technique is to 'take data from clients, and we do some of our own to see if we kind of validate and have a similar set of insights, and if we come up with anything new or a different way to look at it'. Being open and curious is the key to this because if you have the wrong data, you'll get the wrong insight and that will lead to ideas that don't surprise the very people you are trying to attract. Rolfe told me that to get to a unique point of view on a brand you have to get great insight from the data and from understanding people. This allows you to find an intersection between a brand's positioning and your unique point of view and this is where creative magic is most likely to happen.

Rolfe takes this idea further by telling me that she can come up with ideas that work 'really quickly if I have a great insight' but if she doesn't then she 'could have all the time in the world for the actual ideation process, and never get anywhere'. So to make data and creativity in our ads work we need to let 'planners compress and creatives lateralize', as Faris Yakob puts it.

Where ideas come from

In my conversation with Jess Burley she explained that by respecting that ideas can come from anywhere, her agency created a framework to tease out ideas from different sources. The idea here was that each team member had their own expertise and brought something new to the table to encourage cross-collaboration. This decreased the dependency on people with 'creative' in their title. Her agency searched for inspiration in four areas: Consumer Insights, Product Quality, Capability and Ambition. She gives the example of Apple as an organization where 'you would find an insight about the Ambition of Apple, as well as its products and its consumers' and the last stone to turn over is Culture of the business. Burley's advice is to ask, 'Is a business setting out an agenda for change or something unique about their culture that allows you to find an idea?'

Burley's goal here is to create cross-fertilization and collaboration amongst her people whilst taking inspiration from different data sources. This approach of creating as many chances of striking gold as possible is logical but, I assume, time consuming. She's adamant that the creatives aren't the only people who can come up with the ideas, and that inspiration might strike 'the guy that's in the analytics department... or it might come from the strategist.' For Burley it's about respecting each other's crafts and perception of different data sources. And this approach fosters collaboration, helping Burley know that 'More minds are better than one mind, and therefore you're going to get better work.'

When data is the idea

Another angle on using data in the pursuit of creative magic is to just make the data the creative idea itself.

In 1958 Ogilvy did a print ad for Rolls Royce with a headline, 'At 60 miles an hour, the loudest noise in this new Rolls Royce comes from the electric clock.' This is a single data point about the product which is turned into a creative idea. According to Jenkins (who recounted the story to me) it significantly increased sales of the car. He finds this example intriguing: 'So think of all the things people consider when they're buying a car. The volume of the clock is not one of them. But that single data point said more about the quality of the car than anything else you could have claimed creatively.'

Another case study he shared with me was from Argentina, for Heinz ketchup, where they worked out it takes about five-and-a-half seconds to find a bottle of ketchup and pour it. So the agency observed that on average people in the market like ketchup three times a week. They then made the calculation that 'Based on how old someone is they could work out how much of their life they have spent waiting for ketchup to come out of bottles' and they turned it into a print campaign showing people differently just pouring ketchup out of bottles. It says, '65 hours of his life waiting. It has to be Heinz.' Like Rolls Royce, the data itself is the idea and says something about the quality of the product. Jenkins concedes that it is not the most 'high tech' use of data, but it's a 'surprising piece of data that no one really knew before'. And surprise is what we are after when coming up with advertising creative. If we don't surprise we don't stand out; if we don't stand out we don't get noticed; if we don't get noticed no one remembers us and if no one remembers us at the point of purchase – we don't sell.

Jenkins is also a fan of Chipotle, who ran an email campaign where they matched customers who had matching orders elsewhere in the country. The brand would email each matching pair to say, 'There's someone else who orders exactly the same way you do' like 'double lettuce, mild cheese'. This simple idea led to a big jump in email opens and clicks increasing, ultimately earning Chipotle around extra revenue.

What data point does the brand you represent have just sitting there quietly and unnoticed that could be your next idea?

Leap and the net might appear

The examples above give the impression that the idea came directly from the data when in actual fact it is a creative person's idea to make it look like that. A human still had to have the idea to use this data as the idea. In my research I've not found a way around this; at some point you have to take the creative leap yourself or pay someone to do it. As Jenkins puts it, 'The data is just there to kind of tell you, right, this is the situation. But I'm not going to tell you what you should do. It may be quite heavily implied in the data, but it doesn't tell you.'

Lex Bradshaw-Zanger tells us that the time to get creative is 'when you've got that data, then you need to get to a bit of intuition and a bit of creativity and a bit of taking the insight just that step further'. He talks about a point where you 'get to the end of the data and what it's going to give you and then you jump into the creativity'. This view is contrasted by Beecher, who says, 'There's not a point where data stops and creativity starts.' Echoing this view is Jim Sterne. I asked him, 'When's the right time to ditch the data and start being creative?' to which he said, 'Always. Always be creative.' Sterne's view is that 'Data is the support, data is the input. The input is staring out to sea over a weekend and standing in the shower and having a great idea. Input is being at a classical concert and for some reason it reminded you of something from your childhood and you had a great idea.'

If this is all too fluffy and intangible for you, then Ceci Dones offers a pragmatic solution. Her advice is that utilizing intuition-based decision making (or ditching the data) makes sense when everyone agrees that either: 1) there just doesn't exist enough quality data to inform the decision the leader wants to make, or 2) the leader is comfortable enough with the risks of making a courageous, bold bet where there is no data to inform the risk. She concedes, 'As a data person, this might be blasphemous, but under the conditions that the risk is low and you can add experimentation to gather data on whether it is working quickly, I recommend just trying it.' Dones believes that 'It really only takes one creative idea to be brilliant. The data and technology are how we choose to scale the creative idea.'

There's no safety in numbers

My biggest learning from writing this book was that our tendency as an industry is to use data as a crutch and as a way to fit in with what everyone else is doing. It's safety in numbers, literally. One marketer who stands firm against this position is Sinem Kaynak, who told me, 'It's not about ditching the data. It's about having the courage to do what's polarizing. I think that's real creativity.' Drawing from her extensive experience she reminisced about a time when ads across various categories became indistinguishable without their brand logos. This sameness, a safe harbour in marketing, seldom broke new ground. In contrast, she admires brands that take a polarizing stance and which, despite controversies, have garnered a devoted following. These brands' success, she noted, stems from daring to stand for something, a testament to creativity's power when coupled with data to support bold decisions.

'Creativity is subjective, It's good to be polarizing,' she emphasizes, adding, 'It's better to be a brand that actually has that type of advocacy that it stands for something.' In her view, true creativity involves embracing data to fuel decisions that may divide opinion but will ultimately define a brand's identity. She posits that humour, much like creativity, is not universal, but its effective use in advertising can reveal a brand's unique character.

Using AI for ideas

Kaynak has experience in using AI-powered insight generation tools to develop new product concepts for her innovation pipeline. Her approach was to use tools that analysed vast online data sources like consumer reviews, discussions and industry reports to propose new product ideas. Kaynak would rely on the tech to suggest new concepts, describing potential products that could be created. She took these AI-generated concepts and tested them using a more traditional quantitative concept-testing method with consumer surveys. The recommendations and rankings for the most promising ideas that the AI tool proposed closely matched what was found when Kaynak conducted the manual quantitative concept testing. This validated the effectiveness of using AI to identify innovation opportunities without requiring extensive initial consumer research.

There were several benefits Kaynak observed from leveraging AI in the concept development and testing process. It significantly accelerated the generation of new product ideas by surfacing concepts rapidly without the delays associated with traditional upfront consumer research. This faster ideation allowed for more efficient use of resources in innovation. Additionally, the close alignment Kaynak witnessed between AI recommendations and manual testing convinced her that the machine's suggestions could be trusted. While not removing the need for humans to give it the thumbs up, the predictive accuracy boosted confidence in AI's ability to identify potentially successful products upfront. Over time, as the technology continues to learn, Kaynak believes AI may enable certain traditional steps to be bypassed, though integration with consumer feedback remains important. Overall, AI delivered time and cost savings for innovation through streamlined concept generation and validation of its predictive capabilities.

Kaynak's experience demonstrates real innovation and courage in using data and creativity in marketing. Her belief is that data should push us towards bold, stand-out and more meaningful creative. This view is echoed by Cosad, who said, 'Really the question that we're always asking ourselves, and it's kind of exhausting to keep doing it, but it's really important, is – where's the novelty?'

So keep asking yourself, is the data helping your creativity stand out or fit in? Are you being polarizing or just copying what is popular?

Testing your idea as you develop it

Jon Williams' approach at The Liberty Guild is to combine two important data sets. One data set is the collective experience of a large group of celebrated creative directors and real people's reactions to ideas measured in the form of purchase intent. To go into a little more detail, Willams sources ideas from a group of senior and award-winning creative talent and then tests those concepts with the audience before they go to the client. For him it's all about understanding consumers' reaction to the work that aims to 'direct and guide the creative development'. Williams' take is that there's 'a better way of informing creativity than just ego, which is subjective, and if you let the data guide it, you get to a much better place'.

Williams' first step is to share 'an idea articulation' with the target audience in the form of 'ad-shaped things'. The target consumers 'will be able to respond and react' and this gives Willams a read on what they may react well to later in the process. This initial run of creative helps his team whittle down the long list of ideas to three strong concepts to develop. Once these ideas are 'something that's a lot closer to what we'll run' they get shown to the target audience again.

At this point Williams will have presented three worked-up ideas that have been tested for 'purchase intent'. This specific data point is crucial for Williams, who staunchly suggests that if you can win a Cannes Lion then 'well done' but what most clients want is 'something that's going to be effective and deliver on sales'. At the time of writing Williams and his team had data back on sales for a flour brand they worked with in the United States. His approach of removing creative ego and guesswork had contributed to a spike in sales.

Williams concludes that 'We listen to the data as we're going', never working entirely on a hunch. This means that 'We might have been stood in front of the client going, "This is a great creative idea" and the client would believe you or not'. But Williams brings 'a tonne of research that backs that up and demonstrates that this will result in sales. It gives the client confidence to buy braver work.'

Williams' effective approach is not complicated, but it's not commonplace.

Dones' take on this is that all too often 'no one brings back the voice of the consumer'. In her capacity as an academic crossed with a marketing person her students have taught her to ask, 'Is this going to be cringe?' This approach doesn't use reams of Excel sheets but Dones suggests that as you are 'working through the ideas in the creative process' you need to make sure that there is 'some kind of feedback, some kind of signal coming from the consumer to make sure "Hey, is this gonna resonate at all, is this gonna be cool?"'

Don't post-rationalize (and don't cheat)

In my experience at agencies, one of the most disingenuous practices I saw was for a creative person to come up with an idea that they liked and then get the strategy team to justify it with data they found. This is what Rolfe calls 'bad behaviour within the industry' and we 'shouldn't be revalidating an idea to try to make it make sense'. This is the opposite of combining data and creativity; it is in fact ignoring the data and coming up with something randomly. Rolfe goes on to call this 'almost a disservice, just trying to get to an interesting execution or creative idea that isn't necessarily rooted in anything'.

Rolfe's antidote to this dodgy practice is 'staying close to the strategic process, asking questions, going deeper into the data, making sure that those things are true, and not taking it for face value' and not getting caught up in 'having an execution in your head that you think is cool, that you want to do'. Rolfe is adamant that you need to ask if your idea is actually solving a need and is it 'solving a real challenge? Is this connected into a truth?' I concede that advertising is the business of selling, but there's no need to oversell and spin a lie when the world is abundant with data – that can give us a deep insight into the audiences we seek to engage. I guess it's human nature to want to find shortcuts and I'm guilty of it myself.

When creativity dies

Another popular way of cutting corners is to use tech to create all of your ideas for you. At the time of writing there are many services that can generate ideas at speed and scale. Burley sees these technologies as having the ability to support creatives in delivering stronger creative work: 'What it doesn't do is replace the ideation process that the human brain delivers. It can't do that. Maybe down the line.' Her view is that the actual work of coming up with the 'master asset' still 'requires humans' and that tech is there to 'test multiple routes much more quickly than we would have done previously, in order to get to the best possible asset'.

Jenkins warns that we can take data too far. His view is that 'We've all got kind of access to everything', which puts marketers in the quandary that all the competing brands can come up with similar answers and ultimately similar ads, which defeats the point. At the time of writing the industry is in a mild panic about AI and Jenkins sees a world where people 'prompt and reprompt and reprompt in a way that extracts something out down the line – who knows what it's going to be?'

Jenkins warns that if this continues and the same data sets feed the same AIs for similar brands then 'there can be a point where creativity just dies'. So much of advertising is regurgitation of the same ideas delivered in a way that helps brands fit in with their category and not stand out. The promise of AI is to speed up this process and scale it. This is a one-way ticket to a sea of sameness where all advertisers look the same and act the same, even more so than they do already.

REAL-WORLD EXAMPLE

The ALS Ice Bucket Challenge

I'll close this chapter talking about the 'ALS Ice Bucket Challenge' which was a viral social media campaign where participants dumped a bucket of ice water over their heads to raise awareness and funds for ALS research, often nominating others to do the same. This was a viral phenomenon that had nothing to do with data or advertising, but was a 'fun, hyperbolic expression of support' that would likely have been less successful if it had been more of a brand play. Aaron Howe felt the Ice Bucket Challenge was fascinating because it was an example of something that 'would never have been approved' by data or advertising strategies, yet it became a huge success. Howe sees it as an example of how sometimes the most successful campaigns are those that don't heavily feature branding or logos, as people are more likely to engage and share content that doesn't feel overly branded. Howe believes the Ice Bucket Challenge illustrates how data and advertising strategies can sometimes miss or overlook the types of content that resonate most with people in an authentic, viral way.

The ALS Ice Bucket Challenge story highlights why this industry is so interesting to those of us lucky enough to work in it. My take is that you can crunch all the data you like, observe your target, immerse yourself in their lives and be a 24/7 empath but sometimes an idea comes from seemingly nowhere. And that idea could travel further than you could ever imagine.

KEY TAKEAWAYS

- Never let data limit you. Use it as fuel to break rules, not follow them.
- Best-practice thinking is plain old copying – be the brand that surprises everyone.
- Get comfortable going where the weirdness is. Data can hide the best ideas in plain sight.

Conclusion

For years, brands relied on gut instinct, hoping their ads would stick. Now, data gives us a way to see what works and why. It helps us understand people better, what they feel, need and respond to. But data alone isn't enough. The best marketing happens when data and creativity work together.

At the heart of balancing creativity and data is *curiosity*. If you're not curious about your audience then you won't find the insight that sparks creativity that stands out. And if you're not curious about how to come up with new ideas then you're not being creative, you're copying. Stay curious, go where the weirdness is and you'll find that data and creativity start to work together in ways you may not have expected.

So let's put ourselves in the shoes of the people we're trying to reach. Let's find data that taps into the truth about their lives so our creative is relevant and surprising. The best ads make the audience feel something but let's first at least try to feel what they feel.

We see around 10,000 messages from brands every day, and we may react to a few. The rest are ignored, skipped or forgotten. The reason for this is that most brands play it safe, following the same codes of the category, hoping that if they show their ad enough times, the message will slowly seep in. That's the slow path to nowhere. It's our job to make advertising entertaining, inspiring or in the very least understood.

This book has explored how data has changed advertising over time, from the early days of tracking consumer habits to the explosion of real-time analytics. We've looked at how brands can use data to spark creative ideas, write better briefs, build stronger teams and measure success in a way that actually matters. But the biggest lesson is this:

The best advertising happens when we balance logic with creativity, numbers with instinct and insight with imagination. Too much focus on data, and the work becomes robotic. Too much focus on creative impulse, and it risks missing the mark. The key is using data to learn, not to limit.

If you've made it this far, you care about doing things differently. If you want to stay ahead, challenge the norm and keep learning, I invite you to join the conversation.

If you want access to the bonus chapters for this book and regular inspiration on data, creativity and ads then head to **AutomatedCreative.net/ DataAndCreativity.** Or if you'd like to join the 'Marketing, Data and Creativity' WhatsApp Group, scan this code with your phone.

If you'd like to hear full interviews from each of the brilliant minds featured throughout this book, search for the 'Shiny New Object' podcast on your platform of choice.

So, this is it, end of the road. Let's quickly recap the core idea and get practical about how you'll actually use this book tomorrow.

FINAL TAKEWAYS

- Data informs great creativity, it doesn't replace it.
- If you're not curious, you're dead in the water.
- Amazing marketing balances creative risk taking and inspiring data.

FURTHER READING

Belk, R W, Sherry, J F and Wallendorf, M (1988) A naturalistic inquiry into buyer and seller behaviour at a swap meet, *Journal of Consumer Research*, 14 (4), pp 449–70

Bernays, E (1923) *Crystallizing Public Opinion*, New York: Boni & Liveright

Creswell, J W (1998) *Qualitative Inquiry and Research Design: Choosing among five traditions*, Thousand Oaks, CA: Sage

Dichter, E (1964) *Handbook of Consumer Motivations: The psychology of the world of objects*, New York: McGraw-Hill

Field, P and Binet, L (2013) *The Long and the Short of It: Balancing short and long-term marketing strategies*, IPA.

Hill, K (2012) How target figured out a teen girl was pregnant before her father did, *Forbes*, 16 Feb, www.forbes.com/sites/kashmirhill/2012/02/16/how-target-figured-out-a-teen-girl-was-pregnant-before-her-father-did/ (archived at https://perma.cc/55JR-TV7C)

Kwakkel, E (2019) The oldest surviving printed advertisement in English (London, 1477) Medievalbooks, medievalbooks.nl/2019/01/24/the-oldest-surviving-printed-advertisement-in-english-london-1477/ (archived at https://perma.cc/4PN6-ZQPG)

Lears, T J J (1983) From salvation to self-realization: Advertising and the therapeutic roots of the consumer culture, 1880–1930. In R Wightman Fox and T J Jackson Lears (Eds) *The Culture of Consumption: Critical essays in American history, 1880–1980* (pp. 1–38) New York: Pantheon

Linden, G (nd) Book excerpt: First pages of the book, https://glinden.blogspot.com/#:~:text=Book%20excerpt%3A%20First%20pages%20of%20the%20book (archived at https://perma.cc/RVJ4-5P2X)

Malefyt, T de W and Moeran, B (2003) *Advertising Cultures*, Oxford: Berg

McDonald, M and Wilson, H (2016) *Marketing Plans: How to prepare them, how to use them* (8th ed.) Chichester: John Wiley & Sons

Merton, R K and Kendall, P L (1946) The Focused Interview, *American Journal of Sociology*, 51 (6), pp 541–57

Ogilvy, D (1963) *Confessions of an Advertising Man*, New York: Atheneum

Ralston Saul, J (1992) *Voltaire's Bastards: The dictatorship of reason in the West*, Free Press.

Scott, W D (1908) *The Psychology of Advertising in Theory and Practice*, Boston: Small, Maynard & Co

Taleb, N N (2007) *The Black Swan: The impact of the highly improbable*, Random House

Van Maanen, J (1988) *Tales of the Field: On writing ethnography*, Chicago: University of Chicago Press

Wikipedia (nd) History of YouTube, https://en.wikipedia.org/wiki/History_of_YouTube#:~:text=YouTube%20is%20an%20American%20online (archived at https://perma.cc/NC5C-FXND)

Yakob, F (2023) *Paid Attention: Innovative advertising for a digital world*, 2nd ed. Kogan Page

INDEX

Looking for another book?

Explore our award-winning
books from global business
experts in Marketing and Sales

Scan the code to browse

www.koganpage.com/marketing

Also from Kogan Page

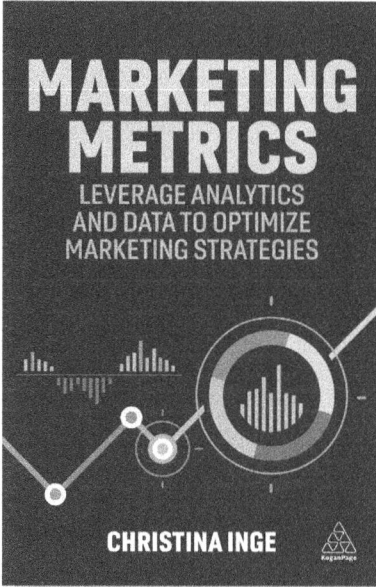

MARKETING METRICS

LEVERAGE ANALYTICS AND DATA TO OPTIMIZE MARKETING STRATEGIES

CHRISTINA INGE

ISBN: 9781398606593

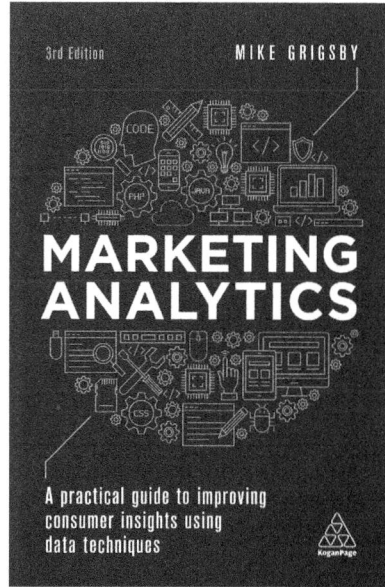

3rd Edition — MIKE GRIGSBY

MARKETING ANALYTICS

A practical guide to improving consumer insights using data techniques

ISBN: 9781398608191

From **Marginal** to **MAINSTREAM**

Why tomorrow's brand growth will come from the fringes - and how to get there first

Helen Edwards

ISBN: 9781398604315

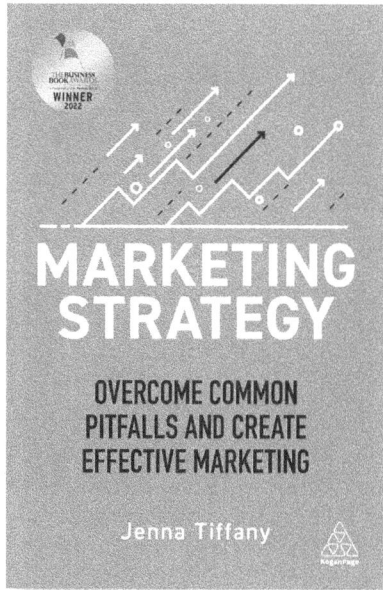

WINNER 2022

MARKETING STRATEGY

OVERCOME COMMON PITFALLS AND CREATE EFFECTIVE MARKETING

Jenna Tiffany

ISBN: 9781789667417

www.koganpage.com

From 4 December 2025 the EU Responsible Person (GPSR) is:
eucomply oÜ, Pärnu mnt. 139b – 14, 11317 Tallinn, Estonia
www.eucompliancepartner.com

9 781398 619258

From 4 December 2025 the EU Responsible Person (GPSR) is:
eucomply oÜ, Pärnu mnt. 139b – 14, 11317 Tallinn, Estonia
www.eucompliancepartner.com

www.ingramcontent.com/pod-product-compliance
Lightning Source LLC
Chambersburg PA
CBHW071602210326
41597CB00019B/3364